John Holmes Acornley

Sunshine among the mountains

or, The young pastor's wife

John Holmes Acornley

Sunshine among the mountains
or, The young pastor's wife

ISBN/EAN: 9783741121616

Manufactured in Europe, USA, Canada, Australia, Japa

Cover: Foto ©Lupo / pixelio.de

Manufactured and distributed by brebook publishing software (www.brebook.com)

John Holmes Acornley

Sunshine among the mountains

Sunshine Among the Mountains:

OR,

THE YOUNG PASTOR'S WIFE:

BEING

MEMORIALS

OF

MRS. AGNES REBECCA ACORNLEY,

WIFE OF REV. JOHN H. ACORNLEY.

BY

HER HUSBAND.

"You may break, you may ruin, the vase, if you will,
But the scent of the roses will hang round it still."

HOWARD DAISLEY, PUBLISHER:
PRIMITIVE METHODIST BOOK DEPOT:
75 Fulton Street, Brooklyn, L. I.
1876.

IN AFFECTIONATE REMEMBRANCE OF

My Dear Wife,

WHO WAS FOR SEVEN YEARS MY DAILY COMPANION
AMID TOILS AND TRIALS,
AND THE SHARER OF ALL MY JOYS AND SORROWS,

THIS HUMBLE TRIBUTE OF LOVE

IS INSCRIBED

BY HER BEREAVED AND SORROWING HUSBAND.

PREFACE.

OF the writing of books there is no end; and some may be ready to ask "Why write another? The world is full of books of this character!" Our only answer is, that Christian biography is an important branch of religious literature, as it affords the devout reader incentives to higher aims and nobler actions.

Christians are said to be like town-clocks; all eyes are turned upon them, and the actions of those who are not Christians are often guided by them. It is as important that the inner lives of quieter and more unobtrusive Christians be held up as examples for the imitation of others, as it is for the lives of greater and more ostentatious men and women to be recorded.

It is not the thunder with all its roar that fells the mighty forest-king—the oak—but the noiseless lightning's flash. The glorious sunshine which is such a powerful force in nature—producing the most stupendous results—comes to us in the most gentle, peaceful, and unpretentious guise. The feathery flakes of snow which thread their way through the atmosphere, as though they were too filmy to yield to the demands of gravity, clothing the earth with a carpet, soft as the most exquisitely wrought brussels, falls softly and silently upon the earth, imparting a charm and beauty to everything visible. The rock which has silently stood the blast of a thousand years; the brook or river which has for ages quietly murmured along its bed; the lovely flowers which grow by the wayside, lifting their tiny petals to the sun, and emitting refreshing odors; the forest with its myriad leaves—nature's mammoth library—all are quietly waiting to impart lessons of wisdom and love.

Thus it is with the lives of virtuous and humble Christians. They may not have taken *leading parts* in life's great drama, but they may have filled some of those minor—though none the less important—places, without which the play would be incomplete. They may not have astonished the world with the thunder of their actions, but the lightning's flash of their virtuous deeds may have leveled some sturdy oak of sin to the ground. They may not have swept over the earth like a mighty rushing wind, or a moral avalanche,

PREFACE.

bearing down the opposing force of hell but like the gentle, glorious sunshine, the unpretentious light of their useful lives has diffused its rays all around; and those rays, insinuating themselves into the charnel house of sin, have filled it with light, and peace, and sweetness, and joy. The record of the inner lives of God's glorified children is the very poetry of our religion. It is the casket of gems they have accumulated—some perhaps, not of the first water—but magnificent gems after all. It is the bouquet of flowers they have gathered—some, perhaps, not the most odorous or pretty—but sweet, beautiful flowers after all. The casket which contains the gems may be rude and unpolished, but it *holds them*. The thread which ties the bouquet may not be of silk, but it *binds the flowers together*.

Thus our work may have been imperfectly accomplished, and some may think that we have given too much prominence to matters of small import; but we believe that " it is lines and shadings and such like apparent trivialities that make all the difference between an expressionless and a life-like portrait." So that even minute matters may, after all, sometimes be worth noting.

We do not claim any literary merit for our work.

PREFACE.

Defects and imperfections it has many. We would therefore ask the indulgent reader to waive severe criticism, and to bear in mind the purpose we have in view, viz: to offer an humble tribute of love in affectionate remembrance of one who has shared joys and sorrows with us, as we have walked together life's uneven path. We also indulge the hope, that this simple recital will be the means of leading some who shall read it, to a nearer acquaintance with our common Lord and Master. May it be so. Amen!

J. H. A.

WILLIAMSTOWN,
DAUPHIN COUNTY, PA.,
July 15th, 1876.

CONTENTS.

CHAPTER I.

PARENTAGE, BIRTH, CHILDHOOD.

Only those who have been pre-eminently notable are by some esteemed—No such material here—In a temple the stones not all alike—More likely to imitate the common lessons of life than the extreme and dazzling—Birth—Parentage—Paisley Abbey—SOUNDING AISLE—MARTYR'S STONE—Preston—Birth-place of temperance movement—Home influences—Child of many prayers.

CHAPTER II.

YOUTHFUL CAREER AND CONVERSION.

Resides with her father's mother—Grandmother's influence and training—Conversion—Such a change in such an individual different to a like change in an old sinner—All sold under sin—Residence with Rev. H. Wheeler—Letters from Miss Baugh—Enters service—Shore Hall—Hollingworth Lake—Found many friends—Letter to Mr. C. Crawford—Rochdale—Favored with occasional services of Methodist celebrities—Anecdote of Rev. John Verity—P. M. minister imprisoned—Commenced a school—Affectionate intercourse with her scholars—Visits Elizabeth C. the child of an infidel—The monotony of daily and nightly teaching not held as an excuse for neglecting Sunday School—Elocutionary powers.

CONTENTS.

CHAPTER III.

COURTSHIP.

Courtship often modestly veiled over in religious publications—If done properly will bear referring to—Extract of letter—consent of parents necessary—Correspondence—A period like this interesting and fascinating to young persons—Extract—Many find pleasure in lavish expressions—Not so her correspondence—Letters—Thoughts about entering the ministry—Letter on the subject.

CHAPTER IV.

MARRIAGE AND SETTLEMENT IN AMERICA.

Marriage—Affection for her husband's family—Family altar—Pecuniary circumstances—Death of her father-in-law—Letter from Rev. John Oscroft—Note to her father—Her husband emigrates to America—Philadelphia—Joins her husband in America—Correspondence—Mrs. Acornley's early impressions of her adopted country—Correspondence—Cheerfulness—Sickness of her child—Joins the M. E. Church—Tamaqua.

CHAPTER V.

AS MINISTER'S WIFE.

Enters the ministry—First appointment—Mount Carmel—Watchful interest in the Society's progress—Church burnt—Benevolent tavern keeper—Letter from Mrs. George—Annual Conference—Removal—Wyoming—First missionary—Mineral Wealth—False impressions—Miners—Religion flourishes—Moral sunshine—Miner's song—Mrs. Acornley eminently fitted for minister's wife—A good minister's wife a benefit to the community—Qualities she ought to possess—Baptist magazine—Good taste—Love of flowers—Affection and peace in her home—Baby's death—Feeble health—purposes visiting England—Disappointment—Extracts from correspondence—Maternal anxiety—Accident to her father—Kindness of friends—Wooden wedding—Surprise party—Morris Run—

Hearty welcome—Sickness—Childish comfort—Bread cast upon the waters—Band of Crusaders—Acts of kindness—Her religion of a practical character—Fond of singing.

CHAPTER VI.

SICKNESS AND DEATH.

Fourth of July—Anxiety to see the Sunday School children—Offers her child to God in baptism—Taken sick—Gradually worse—Last conversation with her husband—Her father and sister sent for—Husband took sick—Anxiety of friends—Mind wanders—Intense suffering—Passed away—Gone to be with Jesus—Our loss great—Letter from brother William—Funeral.

CHAPTER VII.

REMEMBRANCE AND CONDOLENCE.

The wise man's description of a virtuous woman—Watchful Providence—Sweet thoughts of comfort—Letters of sympathy—Preamble and Resolutions adopted by Good Templars—Letters of condolence—Longing to see the land of our birth—Set sail—Arrival in England—Encouragement and sympathy—FINIS.

CHAPTER I.

PARENTAGE, BIRTH, CHILDHOOD.

" Yes, 'tis our duty, and our interest too,
  Such monuments, as we can build, to raise."

" How then shall I begin, or where conclude,
  To draw a fame so truly circular?"

" 'Tis paradise to look
On the fair frontispiece of Nature's book:
If the first opening page so charms the sight,
Think how th' unfolded volume will delight!"
Dryden.

IN reading the lives of individuals some persons esteem only such worthy of perusal as have been pre-eminently notable, such as great warriors, statesmen, travelers, philosophers, philanthropists, and inventors; or, someone profound in learning, high in fame, deeply pious, or notoriously wicked; in short, such as have done something which will dazzle the eye, tickle the ear, or produce a sensation in the feelings. The subject of the following pages, however, formed material for no such memoir. The life of a plain, but earnest young Christian woman is the matter to be brought under review.

In a magnificent tabernacle or temple the stones are not all exquisitely carved, yet the plain ones are calculated to fill useful positions. They are not all great stones, yet the small ones cannot be dispensed with. They are not all in the front, or on the outside of the building; there are many obscure and hidden ones, all of which have been fashioned by labor, and appointed to a useful place. The Great Creator, in his wise economy of nature, has seen fit to make more pebbles than diamonds, and more grasses than flowers. Human beings find that it answers their health better to drink more freely of water than nectar, and to eat more heartily of bread than sweetmeats and confectionery. So the common lessons of life are really what we are more likely to imitate than the extreme, dazzling, and extraordinary lives of persons of which there may be but one in an age, or a few in a nation.

My dear wife, whose maiden name was Agnes Rebecca Whillock, was born April 21st, 1847, in the town of Paisley, Scotland. Her father, the Rev. Benjamin Whillock, was a Primitive Methodist Minister, who preached in a hall which was part of the old abbey; another part being used as the parish, or old abbey church. A portion also lay in ruins. The walls of said ruins were not many feet high. One wing of the building was occupied as dwellings, while what had been built as a private chapel, a kind of wing of the abbey church, went by the name of the *Sounding Aisle.* This chapel had been built and dedicated to St. Mirren by James Crawford, of Kelwynnet, burgess of Paisley, and Elizabeth Calbraith his wife. It was endowed by its founders, with salary for priests, who were to reside constantly there to perform mass, and pray night and day for the souls of the endowers while time lasted. What has become of the revenue, or the priest, I do not know. When the Scotch reformation resulted in the establishment of Presbyterian instead of Roman Catholic churches, praying for dead people went out of fashion. In this Aisle is the tomb of Marjory Bruce, or, as she was called, on account of a defect in her eyes, Queen Blearie, who died from a fall she sustained while hunting near Paisley.

"In 1160, or 1164, Walter founded the abbey of Paisley for Clunic monks from Wenlock in Shropshire, England, from whence he came. The motives which induced Walter to build Paisley Abbey may be gathered from the charter of the foundation of that place, from which we extract the following:—'Know all present and to come, that I, Walter, son of Allan, steward of the king of Scotland, for the soul of King David, of King Henry, and of Earl Henry, and for the souls of all my parents and benefactors, and for the salvation of the body and soul of King Malcolm, and of myself, to the honor of God, and by the power of his grace, shall establish a certain house of devotion below my lands at Paisley, according to the order of the brethren of Wenlock; that is, according to the order of the monks of Clugny.'"

In the Paisley cemetery, behind the martyr's church, is the *Martyr's Stone*, from which we learn, that the bodies of James Agie and John Park lie here, who suffered at the cross of Paisley for refusing the oath of abjuration, February 3d, 1685.

> " Stay, passenger, as thou goest by,
> And take a look where these do lie
> Who for the love they bare the truth,
> Were depriv'd of their life and youth.
> Tho' laws made then, caused many die
> Judges and 'sizers were not free
> He that to them did these delate,
> The greater count he hath to make:
> Yet no excuse to them can be,
> At *ten* condemn'd, at *two* to die,
> So cruel did their rage become.
> To stop their speech caused beat the drum
> This may a standing witness be
> 'Twixt Presbyt'ry and Prelacy."

The town of Paisley, which is also noted for the manufacture of superior shawls, claims the honor of being the birth place of the Rev. Colin Campbell McKechnie, the distinguished and able connexional editor.

Mrs. Acornley's mother, whose maiden name was Caroline Lea, was a native of Preston, Lancashire, England. Preston is a•large manufacturing town on the banks of the river Ribble. "Here the temperance movement took—about forty years ago—that definite form which now passes under the name of Teetotalism, a term which, although by no means euphonious, and resulting from a stammering articulation, covers a principle which, while physiologically sound, and in harmony with the teachings of the word of God and the material and moral well-being of man, is commending itself increasingly to the judgment of statesmen, patriots, philanthropists, and Christians generally." Here, also, the Rev. George Lamb, one of the stalwart pillars in the Primitive Methodist Church, first saw the light of day.

Miss Lea was converted when quite young, and became a member of the Primitive Methodist Church, Saul Street, of that town. She was an intelligent, warm-hearted, pious young person.

In July, 1846, the Rev. William Antliff (now D.D. and Principal of the Sunderland Theological Institute) united her in the bonds of holy wedlock to the Rev. B. Whillock. The following day the young couple bade an affectionate farewell to their friends, and departed for Paisley, their new ministerial station. This part of the south-west of Scotland had an atmosphere damp and foggy. Mrs. Whillock manifested symptoms of asthma, accompanied by a cough which (a few weeks before the birth of her who afterwards became Mrs. Acornley) resulted in the breaking of a blood vessel in the lungs. Medical aid was called in, and medicine of an astringent nature administered. While this stayed the discharge from the lungs it increased the cough; the maternal time of anxiety came on, and the lives of both mother and infant hung in doubt; yet the good Lord brought them both through. Nevertheless the mother endured a continued affliction. The climate was deemed against her health, therefore the Annual Conference complied with a request from Mr. Whillock to remove him from Scotland. However, her health was never perfectly restored. She died at Wrexham, North Wales, and was interred in the Baptist Cemetery, where an inscription on her grave stone will briefly tell her character and death:

UNDERNEATH
lie the mortal remains of
CAROLINE,
LATE WIFE OF BENJAMIN WHILLOCK,
Primitive Methodist Minister,
She was born December 13th, 1823,
and, after a
protracted affliction, departed this life
JULY 13TH, 1849.
Through the blood of Christ she knew, whilst young, that her sins were forgiven, and in death the faith of Jesus gave her assurance, resig-
nation, and peace.
As a Wife she was affectionate and dutiful.
As a Mother firm and kind.
As a Christian steadfast and unassuming.

For some years before Mrs. Acornley's birth her parents had been practical total abstainers from all intoxicating drinks, and so continued; thus, as a matter of course their child was led in the paths of true temperance, hence she became a life abstainer, and as her years increased, temperance principles, meetings and successes became subjects of great interest to her.

Prior even to her birth her parents besought the Lord to accept the child as a living servant and sacrifice, and ever afterwards she was the subject of many supplications. From the first at home, and among her other associations she was encircled with a chain of religious circumstances. Thus she heard of heaven and learnt the way. At an early date she was taught the personal duty of prayer, and was led to realize that

> " Prayer is the Christian's vital breath,
> The Christian's native air,
> His watchword at the gates of death,
> He enters Heaven with prayer."

As a matter of course appropriate passages of Scripture were committed to memory, such as the following words of the wise man, which were taught her as part of her morning and evening prayers:— "Two things have I required of thee, deny them me not before I die, remove far from me vanity and lies; give me neither poverty nor riches, feed me with food convenient for me, lest I be full, and deny thee, and say who is the Lord? or lest I be poor and steal, and take the name of my God in vain." Prov. ch. xxx, 7-9.

CHAPTER II.

YOUTHFUL CAREER AND CONVERSION.

> " 'Tis not for man to trifle. Life is brief,
> And sin is here.
> An age is but the falling of a leaf—
> A dropping tear.
> We have no time to sport away the hours;
> All must be earnest in a world like ours.
>
> " Not many lives, but only one have we—
> Frail, fleeting man!
> How sacred should that one life ever be—
> That narrow span!
> Day after day, filled up with blessed toil,
> Hour after hour, still bringing in new spoil."
>
> Dr. Bonar.

IN after time domestic circumstances in Mr. Whillock's family rendered it expedient, during girlhood, for Agnes to live considerably with her father's mother, Mrs. Tranter, who was a member of the Primitive Methodist Society in Birmingham. Through her grandmother's influence and training she was early taught the duty of "Searching the Scriptures," punctuality at the Sunday-school, and attendance at the services of the sanctuary. Who can fully estimate the moral and spiritual power of such surroundings? In this case the labor was not in vain. Such was her affectionate attachment to her dear grandmother, that her young mind was readily opened to receive those lessons of wisdom and piety which that dear aged grandparent was constantly imparting. And in after years she would look back to this time and speak of it as being the happiest period of her youthful career. When she was about eleven years of age there was a religious awakening among the Primitive Methodists in Birmingham, and it was at this time and place when she professed (with other young persons) to venture her all on the Atonement of Christ, thus rendering her heart and life to Jesus. No wonder now that her affection for the courts of God's house became more fervent; but, in such a case as hers, the change called conversion did not contrast so much with her previous life, simply because of her youth, and her former religious and moral habits and associations. Such a change in such an individual is of course very different to a like change in an old sinner, whose life has been far from righteousness, who, when he is translated out of the kingdom of darkness into the kingdom of God's dear son, becomes a wonder to many, and also to himself. Yet whether it be the young or the aged, the moral or the profane, the Sabbath-scholar or the street Arab, the fifty pence debtor or one who owes five thousand talents, each is under condemnation, all are sold under sin, every one is guilty before God. As none can be justified by works, all need the new birth unto righteousness, and except they are converted and become as little children they cannot enter into the kingdom of God. From this time her attachment to God's house deepened, and she manifested a growing interest in the Sunday School. This formed, to a certain extent, her character, and influenced to a considerable degree her future career.

Subsequently to this she resided with her uncle, the Rev. Henry Wheeler, while he was stationed at Macclesfield. Cheshire, with whom a true Christian feeling ever after subsisted, as will be seen by extracts of correspondence from Mr. Wheeler in a subsequent page.

Mrs. Acornley had correspondence with many friends during her youth, but seeing that we do not possess those letters she dispatched, a few of the answers she received will indicate the character of her friends, and the nature of the correspondence. One or two extracts will illustrate. A pious young woman, residing at Dawley, Shropshire, was one among her acquaintances. On the 20th of April, 1863, Miss Baugh wrote:

" My very dear and affectionate friend :

. . . . . " I am so very glad to hear that you are among kind friends, and that you are so happy. There is an old proverb which says

'In the fear of the Lord there is strong confidence; and his children shall have a place of refuge. Commit thy way unto the Lord, and he shall direct thy path.' When I go to school I feel very strange. I seem to look—and to look—for one who is not to be seen there; but when I am at home I can look at the shadow (meaning her portrait), but the substance is gone, and when I am so busy, you sit there and never say shall I help you, and yet I get on better when I see and think about you. . . . . . Hoping you are well, ... I beg to remain,

"Your ever dear and affectionate friend,
"M. M. BAUGH."

Another letter from the same young lady, dated May 18th, 1863, commenced

"My very dear and affectionate friend:

. . . . . "I hope that you are in the enjoyment of health, also your cousins; please to give my kind regards to them, also to your uncle and aunt. I should be very glad to see them and you—perhaps we shall see each other sometime on earth—if we do not, we may meet in Heaven, when we shall range the sweet plains on the banks of the river, and tell of his love for ever and ever. Dear Agnes, I hope you do not think of giving up your class meetings; remember it is the best place to get our spiritual strength renewed; be determined to go on in the way of duty, it is the way of safety.

. . . . . "I should like to see, to speak to you, what I have not time to write. I constantly keep a bouquet of flowers by you (portrait). I know you like them, and yet you don't take them. I was very much pleased with those you sent me; I have studied the language of flowers, so I know their meaning. I am very glad to hear that you had such a nice treat, but I am sorry you felt so lonely; if you would have friends you must make yourself friendly; but I advise you to be careful with whom you make friends. Beware equally of a *sudden* friend and a *slow* enemy.
. . . . And now dear friend, my time is nearly gone; I must not conclude however, without begging of you to live close to God. Pray for me, and I will pray for you, and may we both improve the grace given, leaving the things that are behind and pressing forward to those that are before, and may it be ours to hear the welcome plaudit. 'Come up hither; inherit the kingdom prepared for you, from the foundation of the world.' Farewell for the present, and believe me to be,

"Your ever sincere friend,
"MATILDA MARIA BAUGH."

There was, perhaps, no young person in the Dawley Primitive Methodist Society more pious than Miss Baugh; she was modest, unassuming and virtuous. She became a married woman, and disease and death soon made her their victim.

Mrs. Acornley wrote Miss Baugh's mother a letter of condolence, as may be inferred from the following extract from Mrs. Baugh, dated May 17th, 1866:

" Dear Agnes :

. . . . . "I was glad to hear from you; your kind letter comforted me more than I have words to express, for my loss was very great; but it pleased the Lord to remove her to himself. Although it is hard to say 'Thy will be done,' yet it may be all for the best in the end ; He had some wise purpose in view that we are not permitted to see now, but we shall know hereafter. I am greatly comforted to know that she is gone to Heaven, where the wicked cease from troubling, and the weary are at rest. She died shouting 'Victory!' or, rather, she asked her father to do so. I should have liked you to have been there to have heard her talk; you would have wondered where she could have found so much to say. It was a pleasure to wait on her, she was so patient and thankful for all we did for her. . . .

"All join in love to you.

"I remain your sincere friend,

"JANE BAUGH."

Some time afterwards, feeling a wish to put forth a laudable individual effort for independent personal maintenance, she answered an advertisement, which resulted in an engagement as nurse-maid in the family of Dr. Collier, of Shore Hall, near Rochdale, Lancashire.

Within sight of Shore Hall is a sheet of water, covering *ninety acres* of ground, called Hollingworth Lake. It was originally constructed as a feeder for the Rochdale and Manchester canal. It is, however, no longer necessary for that purpose. The lake is now owned by a company who have laid out its surroundings as a pleasure resort, and although the scenery cannot be said to be grand, yet Hollingworth Lake is not without its merits. During the summer months and on gala days, thousands of eager pleasure-seekers flock to this place from all parts of South Lancashire and the East Riding of Yorkshire. The bosom of this placid water is dotted with pleasure-boats and racing-skiffs, cutters, and canoes; while every once in a while is heard the shrill whistle of the little paddle steamer as she goes snorting round the lake, or merrily glides across from one landing-stage to the other. The lake is fringed by numerous establishments where candies and toys are dispensed, and where materials for fortifying the stomach and pleasing the palate, are dealt out to those who are willing to pay. Joyous sounds, merry laughter, and sweet music, come rippling over the water, while scenes of gaiety are beheld all around. Some poet has said, while viewing the placid waters of Hollingworth Lake by moonlight,

"Oh, that this peacefulness might long endure,
This lovely scene continue, free from mist!
Who would not seek for what is true and pure?
Who would in aught unbeautiful persist?

"None but the gross and foul who make the earth
A scene of terror, havoc, and distress.
O give us, gracious God, a second birth,
And stem the tide of human wretchedness.

"Give us to love thy works, so bright and fair;
Give us to know where truest goodness lies;
Give, from on high, a living, freshening air,
Before whose current all pollution flies."

While residing in the family of Dr. Collier, Mrs. Acornley soon found many friends, connected with the Primitive Methodist Society at Shore, whose friendship continued and was cultivated for years afterwards. The following letter, which she wrote several years afterwards, will illustrate her sincere attachment to the friends she had made in this place :

"PLAINS, LUZERNE CO., PENN.,
"NORTH AMERICA,

"November 23d, 1873.
"Dear brother Crawford :

"I have long promised to write to you, and the dear, yes, the dear friends at Shore. Oh! how I long to see you all. I watch the plan and see who are the active members at Shore. . . . . .
(Speaking of numerous friends, she says :) Have any

of them removed or gone home to Heaven? How we would like to see you all again. I am going to try to send you a little news, and you will let all my dear friends hear, I know.

"You will hear of us sometimes, I dare say, and know that John is in the ministry, and I believe the Lord owns our efforts. This is the second year that we are on this circuit, and during that time, we have divided into two circuits, and on this part we have built two little churches. . . . . . .

"We are now erecting two more; one will probably be opened in four weeks, and the other, which will be larger, will be opened probably in February or March. . . . . . We have much to be thankful for, though we have many drawbacks. Trade in this part is very bad just now, on account of the great bank suspension; there is not full employment, nor much money stirring. . . . . . yet our members are very kind; . . . . . and now pigs are dying all around, and *dead* pork comes into our buttery, and sausages, mince pies, pork pies, as if we liked them and could eat them. . . . . . I tell you this to let you know we are respected, and among friends; yet I long to mingle with you in England again, at Shore and Rochdale. I do long to see my dear husband's mother and family again; we often feel lonely just because we have no relatives at hand. We have buried our dear little rosebud last July twelve months; his name was Ebenezer Hamer; we felt the Lord had helped us; we have now another son; we call him John Samuel; he is a fine baby, six months old.

"John has been very sick a few weeks ago, but is now better, though not like himself; he has far too much work, the circuit work is heavy, and the local help is insufficient. . . . . . My own domestic cares are many, yet I do what I can in the work; I do not do what I should like, or as much as I wish. Visiting members in this country is not like England, it is up hill and down dale. . . . . . Our circuit extends about twelve miles; we have five places as you will see by the plan I shall send. . . . . . It is only three years since Primitive Methodism was known here, in this Wyoming Valley; it is a lovely part of the country. Winter is now set in in earnest; already the sleighs are out, and the bells on the horses ring merrily. . . . . . I guess if I could see and hear you all reading this it would make me feel like getting my '*bagging*'* along with you; I wish I could; I guess it would be '*gradely*† good.' I shall be hopping in maybe sometime; if not, I trust we shall all meet in the glory land, where the inhabitants never say 'I am sick;' where we shall join in the grand hallelujah chorus to Him that hath loved us, and not only loved us but *washed us* in His own most precious blood; to this end I aspire.

---

* A phrase used in Lancashire for the afternoon meal at four o'clock. † Very good.

"May the Lord bless you all is the sincere prayer of your long lost friend and sister in Christ,

"AGNES REBECCA ACORNLEY."

Shore being in the Rochdale Circuit, and preachers and friends coming and going, her correspondence and acquaintance was extended to Rochdale.

Rochdale is a town of great antiquity, for without doubt it existed as such long before the conquest of Britain by the Normans. The present population is estimated at near 66,000. Rochdale has been favored with the occasional services of many Methodist celebrities, such as John Wesley, Adam Clark, Joseph Benson, Hugh Bourne, Wm. Clowes, &c., &c.

An amusing incident once occurred at an open air service in Rochdale. The Rev. John Verity, while standing on a chair preaching in the street, was accosted by a police officer and commanded to "*move on.*" Mr. Verity very politely said "I hope you will permit me to dismiss the people first?" The officer of course readily assented, when Mr. Verity went into a long explanation as to what he had *intended* to have stated if he had not been interrupted; that it had been his "intention to have told them that Christ had died for sinners, and that they might be saved." And thus he went on for half an hour, telling the people what he had *intended* to have said if he had not been prevented. Meanwhile this "guardian of the law" was expecting, at the conclusion of every sentence, to hear the congregation dismissed, but finding that Mr. Verity's explanation continued to roll on, without any signs of a speedy termination, he turned upon his heel and retired in disgust from the scene.

About the year 1839 the Rev. Mr. Steell, a magistrate, and curate of Littleborough Church, a village about three miles from Rochdale, sent Mr. White, a Primitive Methodist Minister, to prison for preaching in that village, but he was released by the order of George Ashworth, Esq., another magistrate, who rose from his bed at midnight in order to accomplish that object.

There had been a day school kept in the basement of Crawford Street Primitive Methodist Chapel, Rochdale; the school had been so reduced, from some cause or other, that it was discontinued. Mrs. Acornley was requested to make the attempt to recommence it. There was no endowment, no fund for salary apart from what was raised by the individual payments of each scholar. She knew she was young and inexperienced, but had resolved, under God's blessing, to look to her own industry for her living. The task of commencing and establishing a day school, which should afford a livelihood to the school-mistress, from school rates commencing at two-pence per week, required courage, hope, industry and patience; but she attempted and succeeded. In addition to this, she commenced a night school, principally for young women and girls, many of whom during the day were working in the cotton factories, thus being deprived of educational advantages. Her affectionate intercourse with the children endeared her to their hearts, and this was apparent not only in the school-room, and when meeting in the streets, but the absent or sick she often visited at their own homes. An extended acquaintance and friendship thus became established between her and the parents.

There was one little girl named Elizabeth C——, whose father professed to hold infidel principles. This little girl was taken sick; she wished to see her school-mistress, who was also her Sunday-school teacher. The father consenting to such a visit— rather visits might be said, for they were frequent— of course, the conversation and exercises were religous and devout, mingled with prayer and praise; the infidel father was at times much affected, but whether this was from any evangelical convictions, or the natural emotions of a parent who lovingly looked on a sick child, whom he feared would die, it is not for the writer to decide. The child, however, died, and its happy spirit, without doubt, went to mingle with that unnumbered multitude of little ones which stands "around the throne of God in Heaven."

The father's heart seemed broken; life seemed to have lost its charm, and in an incredibly short time, he too, died. May we hope that he has met his child in the glory-land.

Mrs. Acornley was occasionally the recipient of affectionate letters from her pupils, indicative of the kindly feelings and affectionate regard they had for her.

The daily and nightly monotony of teaching was not held as an excuse for not taking share in the labor of Sunday school teaching. On God's day she was active in giving instruction in Crawford street school. Her aptitude for teaching, her religious warmth, her punctual attendance, with her affectionate manner, endeared her to the class she taught.

When tea meetings, festivals, or anniversaries for the school occurred, and recitations, etc., were needed, she was ready to take part. A printed programme lies before the writer, dated Christmas, 1867, in which she was announced to render a piece called "The Crucifixion." This she gave with much feeling, and marked and telling impressions were made. From early childhood, reciting, etc., at Sunday school anniversaries, had been frequently her practice. Her elocutionary powers were somewhat considerable, and it would not be too much to say that her talent in this line was indeed extraordinary.

CHAPTER III.

COURTSHIP.

"Our fortune rolls as from a smooth descent,
And from the first impression takes the bent:
But, if unseized, she glides away like wind,
And leaves repenting folly far behind."
Dryden.

THE subject of courtship—a kind of preface to the larger volume of marriage—is ofttimes modestly veiled over in religious publications, as if it was a circumstance that modest and Christian people should only utter in a whisper to some one particular, confidential friend. The writer thinks that courtship, if properly conducted, will in after years bear referring to and prudently disclosing. In the arena of courtship, not only affection, but conscience, truth, and piety, ought to act their part in undisguised characters. The evangelical motto "Whatsoever ye do, do all to the glory of God," ought to have an application in this interesting practice, as in any other circumstance of life. Such were the feelings and convictions of the writer, and such also were the opinions of her whom "once I courted, now I lament," as may appear from the following extract from her pen, in reply to a letter I wrote her on this subject:

"I felt highly pleased when I read that part of your epistle, stating that 'it would be unwise on your part to allow any rumor, or rather to encourage the same, until (as I understand it), I was made acquainted with your present position and circumstances, also your future prospects in life.' Allow me here to say (I hope I do not flatter you), that a young man of such a frank disposition is worthy of such an one as will honorably and steadily assist him through life, in joy, in sorrow, in prosperity, in adversity. A spirit of such frankness, either in a young man or a young woman is commendable, and deserves a just reward. A frank and upright disposition is honorable, both in the sight of our Heavenly Redeemer and man. . . . . . I pray that the blessing of the Most High may rest upon you, and that the Holy Spirit may direct you in all your undertakings, so that when you have done with the world and its cares, you may be received unto Him who hath washed you, and freed you from the yoke of bondage, is the most sincere wish of

"AGNES REBECCA."

Having settled in our hearts that our affection was mutual and genuine, the next thing was to gain the consent of our parents; if this was withheld, we considered it would be an indication that Providence disapproved, and therefore, all professions or expressions relative to our prospective union, should be neutralized or made void. But otherwise, should they comply, this would be the bugle-sound to give us marching orders to "go forward."

A reference to some of her correspondence at this period may not be uninteresting or unprofitable. Having made her an offer of marriage, the following extract will indicate the intelligent, frank and Christian manner in which she accepted my proposal. Speaking of some recent change in her circumstances, she says:

"But yet I will not repine; it is the will of God; 'let Him do as seemeth Him good.' I yet believe that the sun will again shine upon my path, though I assure you I have passed through much, but I will raise my Ebenezer and say, 'hitherto the Lord hath helped me.' Oh! that I may live nearer to Him who has kept me in infancy and childhood, unto these years, to know and understand right from wrong, good from evil; to live closer to Him is my constant desire—my motto is, 'nearer, my God, to Thee.' He who has been a present helper to many before my existence and since, will be my constant, never-failing friend. Yes! a friend that is more constant than a brother. . . . . . Allow me to say that in *you* I have the firm belief I shall find an earthly friend, faithful and true unto the last. 'Last' you say, 'what does that mean?' It means this: I am not a flirt, nor should I wish to trifle with any one, nor any one to trifle with me; but it is my duty to seek out a fit companion 'for life,' and I would not give my hand nor heart to any young man whom I believed had not the fear of God before his eyes. You have had a good example set before you, and I feel thankful that you have followed the same, and given your heart to Him who is your Heavenly Father. Oh! that you may live closer to your God than you hitherto have done. . . . . . And now let our efforts be joined for the promotion of God's cause. To *you* I now give my *heart*, but not without due and serious consideration. And may the God of *Jacob* be my helper and yours, is the most ardent desire and prayer of *your*

"Most affectionate

"Agnes Rebecca."

The following letter breathes the same kind of pious emotions:

"Dear John:

"I most sincerely hope that you arrived safe at home on Sunday night without taking cold; for I know you must each* have got very wet indeed. This day has been so dull to me, as the morning's

---

* Rev. James Crompton and myself, both having been preaching in the neighborhood.

post brought me rather unwelcome intelligence; but I will look up as well as I can, the Lord helping me. I hope soon to see you, for I do think that I may place confidence in you. . . . . . And, oh! I pray that God may bless you, and that all you do may prosper, both temporally and spiritually; that you may have His choicest blessing resting upon all your goings out and comings in; and whatever station of life you may be placed in, you know there is a watchful eye that neither slumbers nor sleeps, continually over you. Oh! that His arms of love and tender mercy would ever you embrace. I assure you, since I have had the knowledge of you, many have been the prayers that have ascended up to the throne of grace in your behalf.

"I have not thought of *you*, or the circumstances that have transpired, lightly, oh! no! I have pondered it over and over again, and asked my Heavenly Father to direct me in the way that is right, to 'guide me by His unerring counsel,' and you also, so that we may each discern more clearly and aright, what is before us. My dear John, do think before you go any further; oh, consider—do you think I am a suitable companion for you through life? I ofttimes feel my littleness and insignificance in the sight of Him who is all just and holy; He who is my Creator, my Preserver, my Redeemer, and my Mediator. I feel that I am sinful. I feel that I can exclaim 'what am I, that thou art so mindful of me?'

He has watched over me constantly; He has covered me with the shadow of His almighty wing. With Milton, I can seem to say,

> 'I have naught to fear—
> This darkness is the shadow of Thy wing.
> Beneath it I am sacred;
> Here can come no evil thing;'

and then, with a more inspired writer than even he, 'what shall I render unto the Lord for all his benefits?' . . . . . In return, I wish for my life to be more devoted to his service; to do His will shall be my constant delight. Oh! that he may ever help me and you to do His will, so that when He comes to number up His jewels, we may each be even more precious than the most costly; for if the world were brim full of the most precious jewels, they were less than nothing when compared to the value of one soul. . . . . . I hope soon to see you, and meanwhile, I pray, that He who fed the five thousand in the wilderness, may feed you with Heavenly bread; He who shone in the bush may shine around about *you*; and the peace that the world cannot give or take, may ever dwell within your soul. And now accept my kindest love, believing it comes from a sincere heart.

"Most affectionately yours,

"AGNES REBECCA."

The circumstances of a period like this are, to most young persons, very interesting and fascinating; but even at this time my dear departed one did not lose sight of, or forget, the principle taught in the decalogue, viz., "Honor thy father and thy mother," &c., as witness the following communication, which I received in July, 1866. She says—"I am sorry to hear that your mother is so poorly, I do hope and trust that she will be restored *soon* to perfect health; remember *you* must take care of *her*, for the true value of a mother no one on earth knows except those who have lost one. I sometimes think that, could I, I would give all I possessed, and do all that ever lay in my power, if I could call back my own dear parent, or even her who I shall ever think of as a parent, (my dear grandmother); but no I cannot; but there is one thing I can do—'*I* can go to them, though *they* cannot return to me.' Ah! I cannot tell how soon that day may come when I shall see them and my Saviour. Here, by faith, we can see the land that is yet afar off. Oh! my dear John, if God should permit that my life and yours should be spared, and that we should be joined in the holy bonds of wedlock, let us pray that our efforts may be united to promote each other's spiritual interest and eternal welfare. In your last epistle you write 'Agnes, pray for me;' believe me, my dear, that not one night passes over your head but that there is an earnest prayer ascending up to the throne of heavenly grace on your behalf. In return I now ask 'pray for your Agnes Rebecca!' May the Lord ever bless you. . . . . . Believe me to be,

"Most affectionately yours,

"AGNES REBECCA."

While not a few young persons find pleasure only in lavish expressions of an emotional character, or even very nonsense, such was not her mode of correspondence. Here is an instance of a pious reflection on the love and goodness of God, and a kind Providence, at the beginning of a new year.

"January 30th, 1867.

. . . . . . " Near one month of this present year has flown into a vast eternity. How many, since the commencement of the year, have passed away to prove the realities of another world, while you and I have been spared! Let gratitude to Almighty God fill each of our hearts. I feel that I need much of His divine assistance to direct, guide, and strengthen me. My desire is to live the life of the righteous, so that my end may be peace. Oh! my dear, pray much for your Agnes Rebecca. I feel I need some one's prayers, especially yours; you for whom I wish to think as for myself; for whose welfare, temporally and spiritually, I constantly and earnestly pray. May the choicest of God's blessings ever be yours;

may the light of His glory beam ever on your path through life; and, when you have done with earth and all its joys and sorrows, may you be conducted by holy angels and 'spirits of just men made perfect,' to sit down with Abraham, Isaac, and Jacob, there to sing the song of Him who hath redeemed you, 'not with corruptible things such as silver and gold, but with His own precious blood.' I pray we may each look unto Him, knowing that from Him all our blessings flow. How innumerable they are! for, while many are in want of daily sustenance, our wants are supplied; while others have not sufficient to wear to screen them from the inclemency of the weather, we have that which is comfortable and warm; there are those who have not habitation, nor bed to lie down upon, while we each have that blessing.

'Not more than others we deserved,
Yet God hath given us more.'

"Let us each feel we have a thankful heart, and may it be our constant aim to do that which is right in the sight of God. Lord help us. . . . . .

"With affection yours,

"AGNES REBECCA."

There is a pious reflection on my birthday, dated December 27th, 1866.

> "Again appears thy natal day;
> Again with blessings be it crowned:
> In virtue's path, and wisdom's way,
> May'st thou on each return be found."

"Many happy returns of this day to you, my dear John, and may you live to see many, many more. I pray that your future life may be a life of holiness, following your Lord and master with greater vigilance and earnestness, and by faith taking firmer grasp of the hem of His garment. Let your light shine, and be not weary in well doing, knowing that if you waver not, but prove faithful unto the end, there is laid up for you an everlasting palm of victory and a never-fading crown of glory. I pray that your life may be spared, having health and strength to perform the daily task of life; and. oh! should it please God that you and I should be united, I say again, and pray, that our efforts may be joined, not only in things temporal, but to promote God's glory. May God ever bless you is my constant prayer. . . .

"With true affection, I am still yours,

"AGNES REBECCA."

For a number of years my mind had been seriously impressed with the importance of devoting myself wholly to the work of the Christian ministry, an impression which was shared by many of my official brethren; and for the accomplishment of which, hundreds of prayers had been offered by a holy father and a God-fearing mother. It was, however, necessary that our engagement should be protracted during the period of my probation (*four years*); the decision hung in the balance month after month. I conversed with her on the matter in its various relations. She finally signed the official document, promising to wait the prescribed period of probation; and then she wrote me as follows:

"Since you named concerning your going into the ministry to me, my heart has seemed to beat quicker than usual; my thoughts upon the subject have been *serious, various*, and *many*. I do pray that the blessing of God may attend your path, and should you go and proclaim the unsearchable riches of Christ to a fallen world, giving up all for your Saviour and blessed Redeemer, who died to redeem you from the yoke of bondage; I do hope and sincerely trust that you will never be 'weary in well-doing.' Remember the promise of our blessed Redeemer, that: that which ye sow shall ye also reap. *Go*, my dear John, and cast the bread upon the waters, and it shall be seen after many days. *Go*, and proclaim the glad tidings of peace to perishing sinners; tell them of a pardoning Saviour, who died to save even the vilest of the vile, so that when here you have done, and suffered his righteous will, you may be admitted into that Heavenly Jerusalem, there to bear and wave an everlasting palm of victory, and wear a never-fading crown of glory; and in that crown may there be placed many, many stars in remembrance of the souls you have won to Christ while on earth. *Go on*, my dear John, and work while it is called day, work for Christ in his vineyard, and may the Lord ever be your helper. If so be that you and I should be parted for some time, remember that there is one in this 'wide, wide world' who would sacrifice anything that was possible for your temporal welfare. And should it ever prove that you come in contact with one who has a *prettier face, or a brighter looking purse, bear in mind that her love* CANNOT *be more pure, or more sincere than mine.* I shall never wish to stand, or be an obstacle in your way; but, rather, on the other hand, *as help-mate* to help you 'onward, upward, and Heavenward.' May God grant that it may be so. . . . . With kindest love, believe me to be,

"Affectionately, your

"AGNES REBECCA."

"Sept. 5, 1866.

CHAPTER IV.

MARRIAGE AND SETTLEMENT IN AMERICA.

> "Like the wanderer's step in snow,
> Ever be my lot,
> Leaving the trace of the way I go,
> But staining not."

IN the preceding chapter, my contemplated project of entering the ministry as a probationer, has been stated. While it had been for years the desire of my father that I should be so occupied, and had for more than two years been talked of by my religious friends, my betrothed and myself; yet, towards the close of the year 1868, I resolved to get married, thus closing the avenue to the ministry in connection with the British P. M. Conference. Accordingly, on the 17th December of that year, we were united in the holy bonds of wedlock by the Rev. William Wilkinson, in the Primitive Methodist Chapel, Smith street, Rochdale, Lancashire.

In the hearts of all the members of my family, an affectionate feeling for Agnes had sprung up; consequently, when our acquaintance resulted in marriage, they were ready to receive her as my wife with open arms.

My father, who was then (and had been for some years) very sick, was unable to attend and witness the ceremony; but directly it was over, we posted off to receive his congratulations and blessing. Having thus entered upon the duties of married life, and of course wishing the blessing of God on our union and labors, we immediately erected a domestic temple—with a social altar for praise and prayer to our Father-God. Nor was my dear wife simply a silent witness; she often officiated as priestess at this altar, sending up burning petitions to the throne of God.

Neither of us inherited any pecuniary fortune; our estate and capital consisted of our mental and physical energies, developed by our personal industries. With loving hearts and willing hands, we hoped under God's blessing to win a livelihood. She therefore resolved to continue her school, which she did as a select or private one, giving her instructions at home, until failing health compelled her to resign it. Our domestic bliss was somewhat interfered with by the fact that my dear father (who, as I said, had been ailing for many years,) was confined to his bed the very day after our marriage. That affliction lasted six weeks, and then his trials of life were at an end; the Lord Jesus lighted up the valley of the shadow of death with the brightness of His glorious presence; the gates of the heavenly city were thrown wide open, and the internal glories of the paradise of God burst upon his view, and triumphantly stepping upon the shore of everlasting deliverance, his happy spirit was " absent from the body and present with the Lord." While father lay sick, I received a letter from one of our aged ministers who had labored in Rochdale Circuit, the Rev. John Oscroft; that letter had a reference to our marriage and my father's affliction, and may not be uninteresting at this point; I therefore take the liberty of transcribing a portion of it which runs as follows:

"LYNN, Jan. 30th, 1869.

"Dear Brother Acornley:

"I received your note and was glad to hear from you. You say that you have changed your state from single blessedness to matrimonial bliss. I hope you will realize the truth in the fullest sense of the word. It is said 'he that findeth a wife, findeth a good thing,' and if that wife be sanctified by divine grace, she will be the more valuable to her loving and God-fearing husband. Strive together to keep God in the house, for His presence and favors are better than life; it is this alone that constitutes matrimonial bliss. I thank you for the kind manner in which you speak of me in your note. I don't know that I have done anything to make such favorable impressions on your minds, or to call forth such friendly and Christian expressions concerning me. God bless you both. Amen.

"You inform me that your father is now confined to his couch with a severe affliction, from which he may never recover. Under such circumstances, what a consolation it must be to his sorrowing family to learn, in the hour of dissolving nature, that his faith is strong, his prospects bright, his evidence clear, and his hope of glory blooming with immortality! . . . . . My Christian regards to you all. Amen. I am not so well myself; Mrs. Oscroft is tolerable.

"Yours, &c.,

"JOHN OSCROFT."

On the day of my father's death, my dear wife wrote to her own father, informing him of the fact, and as the letter illustrates her Christian affection for my parents, I insert it here.

"February 7th, 1869.

"My dear father:

"I am very sorry to inform you of the death of your old acquaintance and friend, and my dear father-in-law, this day, Feb. 7th, 1869. He died calmly and in the full assurance of a gospel hope. I was with him at the time of his departure, with my husband, dear Mrs. Acornley and William Henry;

we all saw him pass from this transitory scene to prove the beauties and realities of another; may our end be like unto his. He is now spending an eternal sabbath in that 'bright and better land.' We purpose to lay his remains beneath the clods of the valley on Wednesday next, the 10th. My dear father, remember us each at the throne of grace. With love to all, we remain,

"Your affectionate son and daughter,

"A. R. and J. H. A."

In the summer of 1870 we formed the resolution to emigrate to America; consequently, in May of that year, I left my dear wife, with a baby only a few months old, took passage, and after sixteen days' "life on the ocean wave" landed in Boston, and proceeded to Philadelphia, where, in a few months, I was joined by my dear wife and child.

Philadelphia has a population of nearly 700,000, and covers an area of nearly thirty square miles. It has a thousand miles of streets, which are lighted at night by 10,000 gas lamps; to supply those lamps with gas there are over 600 miles of piping, concealed under ground. It has more than 200 miles of city railroads, over which there are nearly 1,800 cars passing every day. There are over 400 public schools, attended by over 80,000 scholars, who are taught by 1,600 teachers. There are over 400 places of worship, which have accommodation for 300,000 persons.

There are nearly 9,000 manufactories, with a capital of nearly 185,000,000 dollars, giving employment to 145,000 persons, the annual product of whose labor is over 384,000,000 dollars. There, in 1776, the Declaration of Independence was signed, and here, in 1876, the Centennial of that event is being celebrated, and the world's great exhibition is being held.

To those unacquainted with the circumstances of the case it may appear strange that we should undertake such a long journey, at separate periods of time, but the reason was, that not being in affluent circumstances, and not knowing whether or not America would be adapted to meet our purposes, we deemed it prudent that I should first try it, and then, if circumstances were favorable, Mrs. A. would follow after. I need hardly say, that at our *re-union* our joys and pleasures were mutual. Previous to her leaving England, she wrote me a number of times. The following extract from two of those letters will illustrate her feelings at this period:

July 8th, 1870.
"My dear husband:

"Or rather, '*house-band*,' when we have no house to bind at present. Your long and loving epistle came duly, and it was truly welcome. . . . . . We were so pleased with the account of your voyage, &c., it was really entertaining. I read the letter after class (I go to yours). James Schofield cried and laughed over it. They all seemed over-joyed, and hope you remember them and the Wednesday night's meeting, as they do you; all of them pray for you, and they wish you to pray for them. We do have such good meetings. Oh, it makes me feel so happy. I hope, dear John, you remember *me* at the throne of divine grace, as I need more of the love of God abiding in my heart—more grace to sustain me. I ever think of you and try to bear you up. May the Lord bless you and me, and our dear boy, and help us to train him up for heaven. He is a dear little creature. I do feel very thankful for the temporal prosperity that has attended you thus far.

"Your loving wife,
"AGNES REBECCA ACORNLEY."

Again :
"August 1st, 1870.

"Mother is so thankful things have resulted so well for you, and so am I. I trust we may do well, be a blessing, and be blessed. Darling baby has been so very sick I was afraid I should have to leave him in Bury Road (cemetery.) I do not know yet how it may turn with him. We are to take very great care of him. I trust he will get well. He is better to-day than for a week past. I have been very ill myself, but am much better to-day. Both of us have had to doctor, and you know it will take something to make me have a doctor, or go to one. I trust I may soon be all right. I think if all is well I shall start for America three weeks next Wednesday. I would start sooner if I could hear of anyone who was going to New York. Mother wants to see how baby is before I decide; it will not do to start until he is better. I will write again as soon as I know the vessel and the date of starting.

"Your loving wife,
"AGNES REBECCA ACORNLEY."

Having made her final arrangements, she left Rochdale. From Liverpool she wrote to her mother-in-law as follows:

"Liverpool, August 24th, 1870.
"My dear mother:
"You will be very anxious to know how dear baby is. He is much better this morning. I do not feel well myself, but hope to be better before the day is out. . . . . . I put my case in the hands of God; he will take care of me and darling. As dear William said last Sunday night at Smallbridge, 'He hath measured the *waters* in the hollow of His hand,' and if I am in His hand what have I to fear. If I am able I will drop a line from Queenstown. I certainly feel very lonely; but it is as well that you did not stay all night, though your company would have been such a luxury, and so acceptable. Give my dear brothers Sam and Fred my love, and kiss them for

me; I do so wish they were here, for I know their little hearts would leap for joy. Give my love to Mary Jane and kiss her, and tell her to try to be a woman, and do what she can for you. Do not forget dear William and Sarah Hannah; tell them I send the *true love of a sister* to them. And now, dear mother, God bless you, we shall soon see each other again; accept the warm love of an affectionate daughter.

"AGNES REBECCA."

Again she wrote the next day:

"Liverpool, August 25th, 1870.
"My beloved mother:

"You will be astonished when I tell you that we are not on board yet. I am nearly tired of a Liverpool life and no Iome. I cannot tell you how fatigued I feel. I have never had darling out of my arms to-day, and have been backwards and forwards to the offices and pier to know particulars. Our luggage is to go on board to-night. I cannot tell you when we shall start I am sure. I was so glad to receive a letter from William this morning, it was quite unexpected, and consequently was so good. Give my love to him and Sarah Hannah, also Polly, Sam and Fred. God bless you dear mother.

"From your loving daughter,

"AGNES REBECCA."

From the above it will be seen that she cherished the idea of seeing my dear mother again. How uncertain is every earthly thing! How little did she anticipate when she wrote, that she had seen her for the last time on earth! How important the injunctions of holy writ, "Set thine house in order," "Be ye also ready," &c., &c.

"Mrs. Acornley's impressions of the land of her adoption were favorable from the first, and she set herself at once to the task of making her home comfortable and agreeable for her husband.

The following, dated September 24th, 1870, is to her father, giving an account of her safe arrival:

"1953 Warnock Street,
"Philadelphia, Pa.

"My dear father:

"I dare say you will wonder why I have not written before now to tell you of our arrival. Well, the reasons have been many, but I feel very thankful to tell you we are safe and getting much better than we have been since our voyage. We had it rough all the way except three days. Baby was under the doctor's care most of the time, and I was sick all the time except the last two days. When I arrived in New York I was very weak. Since I got to Philadelphia I have had the throat complaint. My cough got most violent on the voyage, and is still distressing; but with that exception I feel moderately well. But to alter the subject, Mr. Hamer and John met me at New York; I need not tell you how glad I was to see them. Mr. Hamer seemed quite as anxious as John for my arrival; he met me with the affection of a father; he is truly *a friend*. Well, we started off to Philadelphia, and got here something after midnight. The house is pleasantly situated and convenient; I hardly need describe the appearance of the outside of the house, for now you are in America, I doubt not you have seen far more than I have. I have not been in the city yet; my time has been fully occupied. There are no P. M.'s here. But more another time. Write to us soon.

"Our love to you, dear father, from your affectionate daughter,

"A. R. A."

On the 29th of October, she wrote as follows to my mother:

"1953 Warnock Street,
"Philadelphia, Pa.

"My beloved mother:

"I have plenty of news for you, but I do not know whether I can tell you one half; I am afraid not.

"This city is a magnificent place—you have no idea. There are large shops, (or stores, as they call them here,) hotels, churches, etc. Down each side of the foot-path, in the centre of the city, are shade-

trees growing. Many of the houses are flat-roofed;
we can walk out on the top, dry clothes, etc. There
are plenty of churches, but no P. M.'s. We have
been twice to the Cohocksink M. E. Church, which
is the most like a P. M. Church I know of. In the
afternoon that I went there was an experience meeting—a right lively one too. At night there was a
good sermon preached; they started the prayer-meeting with 'Turn to the Lord,' &c. They conduct their services different altogether. All the
congregation stay at the prayer-meeting. Service
begins at 7.30 P. M.

"John and the rest are away from home, but give
his and my love to all the dear friends at Smith
street and Bamford, if you see them. We are still
yours,
"JOHN AND AGNES."

To her sister she wrote—

"Dear Fanny:

"Ten minutes ago I received a letter from
father for my husband; from it I gather that you
are quite well, also father, but that your mother is
sick. I hope that you will take care of her and
nurse her well, that she may soon recover, and enjoy
better health than she has formerly; give her my
love, and tell her I cherish for her a *daughter's
affection.* How do you like this country? I like it
exceedingly well, though you must not think that all

is smooth, yet I have cause to rejoice. I trust you will feel satisfied in this country, and do your very best to make home cheerful, and your mother and father comfortable. If you do your duty thoroughly you will be repaid. . . . . .

"Wishing you prosperity, temporal and spiritual, with a sister's fond affection, I am still,

"AGNES REBECCA."

She was cheerful and pleasant in the performance of all her domestic duties, and was ever ready with a word of encouragement or sympathy, as the case might be, whenever I returned home from business, weary and downcast. During our residence in Philadelphia she made many friends, for whom she retained a warm affection to the day of her death.

While residing in the city she often suffered intensely. At one time, after speaking of her own sickness, she thus refers to the sickness of her eldest child :—

"Since I have been sick, Benjamin Richard has been taken sick; he has had fits and inward convulsions, which held him from twenty to thirty-five minutes; poor, dear little darling, and me not able to help him. You know what a mother's feelings would be at that time. I thought my heart would break. However, the doctor considers him out of danger now. Praise God!"

As we sought in vain for a Primitive Methodist

Church in Philadelphia, we were at this time worshipping and laboring with the Cohocksink M. E. Church, Germantown Avenue.

Subsequent to this, in order to be more in the midst of my business connections, we removed to Tamaqua, a county town of about 8,000 inhabitants, situated among the mountains of Pennsylvania, a great height above the level of the sea. It is in the county of Schuylkill, and ninety-nine miles distant from the city of "brotherly love." Through its centre runs a little creek, which, as it goes, gathers volume and strength, until, by the time it reaches Philadelphia, it becomes the respectable river Schuylkill. The business of the town is principally coal mining. There is one large iron foundry, a shoe factory, railroad communication with the outer world; and the religious privileges are on a par with other towns. Here we resided until Providence opened the way for our introduction into the work of the Christian ministry.

CHAPTER V.

AS MINISTER'S WIFE.

> "If you have not gold and silver,
> Ever ready to command;
> If you cannot t'ward the needy,
> Reach an ever open hand;
> You can visit the afflicted,
> O'er the erring you can weep,
> You can be a true disciple,
> Sitting at the Saviour's feet.
> *Mrs. Ellen H. Gates.*

Previous to the events recorded in the closing part of the last chapter, I had received an invitation to labor as an itinerant minister in the M. E. Church, and also one from the people of my early choice, (Primitive Methodists) Of course I resolved to identify myself with the latter—the church of my fathers—a determination which my dear wife encouraged. Writing to her mother-in-law from Philadelphia, she says: "While John was in the coal region, he found some P. M.'s, and preached for them; you should just see his excitement over the matter; he says it was a real treat." Referring to the fact of a number of ministers having left the connexion, and the societies being consequently without a shepherd, she says, " John is a member of the M. E. Church, Philadelphia; he will have a licence this year to preach for them, *unless he goes to preach for our dear lost people up in the coal region.*" Again, she says, "A gentleman has had some serious talk with John about the ministry (M. E.) He told John to prepare himself. Our own people at St. Clair are without a minister. . . . . . John is in a strait what to do; will you advise him, mother; his heart is in the work. Pray for us, dear mother, as we do for you.

We entered our first appointment at Mount Carmel, November, 1871. This is a small mining town of about 1,300 inhabitants, very pleasantly situated, in Northumberland Co., Pa. Here Primitive Methodism had struggled for an existence a number of years, services being held in school-houses, and the homes of our people. When we entered the station the foundation of a new church had already been laid, upon which the building was erected during our stay. An extract of a letter to her father will show her watchful interest in the society's progress.

" Mount Carmel,
" Northumberland County, Pa.
"April 10th, 1872.
" My dear father :
"I am sure I wish you many, many happy returns of the day; I trust you will live to see many more.

I had intended to send you $5.00, to arrive upon your birthday, but I did not have it just then. You will find it inclosed. I would like to send more but cannot just now; this may be useful to you. . . . . . I will inclose you bits of dresses the children have had sent them. The people seem to have received us very well here, and our efforts have been crowned with success; to God be all the praise.

"John will give you an account of the revival services. He is not well at all; his chest and throat are very bad; cannot you tell me what might do him good? I have tried many remedies. I think it probable we shall be removed this conference; the circuit extends some thirty or more miles, and we expect it is going to be divided. The conference commences May 1st, at Tamaqua. I shall be very sorry to leave Mount Carmel for many things; but I trust all will be for the best. Good bye; the Lord be with you and bless you is the prayer of

"Your affectionate daughter,
"AGNES REBECCA ACORNLEY."

To her sister, after speaking of the various efforts in behalf of the Church, she says: "I'll tell you we are very busy; the people are exceedingly kind to us. . . . . . I feel that we are going to be the agents for good. I pray that much good may be the result of our efforts, but until there is a change with our dear little one, I cannot get out so much as I did. Try to be a good girl to your dear mother and father; do your duty at all times, in all places; give them each my kind love."

The progress of the work of God was a subject upon which she loved to dwell; and it afforded her intense delight to see sinners saved. To her mother-in-law she wrote, March 31st, 1872: "I am really so delighted with your photograph, 'tis such an exceedingly good one; we are so very glad you have sent us one. John has been away this week holding protracted services that have been going on *three* weeks, and I expect he will be there (Shamokin) next week. He is so happy, they have had such glorious seasons. He came home this morning at 6.15, and went away again in the afternoon at 3.15, for his to-morrow's appointment. So, you see, 'tis quite a luxury to have him home. I should like you to see his journal; I have just been reading it over. It would do you good. I believe, dear mother, the Lord does bless him, and his efforts; and my daily prayer is, 'O Lord, *do* give him souls for his hire and seals to his ministry.' Last Sabbath he preached at Mount Carmel; we had a time of refreshing from the presence of the Lord. *Three* precious souls stepped into the glorious liberty of the sons of God. And *one* went home sorrowing. I trust it will prove sorrow that will work repentance. There have been *thirteen* brought through in the circuit by his agency since he started in the work at Mount Carmel.

Praise the Lord! Oh! it does make me feel so happy. I feel the Master is with him,—with us. . . . . I saw the little glistening drops come when I showed him your photograph. . . . . . I cannot here enumerate the draw-backs we have had, dear mother, but we have had them without number. If dear John has his health we shall yet see better, brighter and pleasanter days; I will not say happier, for we are as happy in each other's confidence as ever we can be; every week seems to make us dearer to each other. I pray that the Lord may spare his life; that it may be a life dedicated to God's service. Oh, dear mother, I cannot tell you how much I love my husband. Do not think me foolish; I have *no one* to tell any one thing to, except him, in this strange land. Though *friends* we have many, thank the Lord! but not one to whom I could tell a trouble or joy. That is one reason why I so much crave for you to be here; for when he is away week after week it is so lonely and dreary, and it makes me feel low spirited; the children are so young and delicate, John does not know how they suffer, he is away so much, and I get weary. But I am complaining, and I do not want to say any thing that will make you feel bad dear mother. The Lord is very good to me amid all the vexations. There are hosts of things I could talk to you about that I cannot write. Our Festival was a success. Accept my love,

"Your ever affectionate daughter,

"AGNES."

During our residence in Mount Carmel a great trial overtook our little society at Girardville. The church, which was worth about $6,000, and had only just been cleared of debt, was burnt to the ground; an organ which cost $300, and the new pulpit bible, which was the gift of a number of young men, were also destroyed, together with a house which stood on the next lot, belonging to sister Weightman. This calamity had a great effect on the mind of sister W. and brought on a long and protracted sickness. This occurred Friday, February 2d, 1872. The friends, although deeply humbled before God, were not discouraged. Their hope was in God, and they believed that

"Behind a frowning providence
He hides a smiling face."

Their faith was honored; for the day following, Saturday, February 3d, a meeting was called to take steps towards erecting a larger and more substantial building. God blessed them in their subsequent efforts, and now a neat brick structure stands on the old site, an ornament to the town, and a credit to the heads and hearts of those brethren whose labors contributed towards its erection. Thus were they enabled to fully realize that

"God moves in a mysterious way
His wonders to perform."

While we sat in consultation as to what would be best to be done with regard to continuing the services during the erection of the new church, God put it into the heart of Mr. Griffiths, the tavern keeper, to allow us the use of a room he had behind the tavern; a messenger was sent to the meeting to inform us of this offer, who also intimated that we should not be expected to pay a single cent for rent. Expressions of joy and gratitude burst from the lips of every one present, and earnest prayer was offered that God in his infinite mercy might bless the man who had thus come to our aid in this time of need. That afternoon the room was filled with benches, and made ready for service. The following day I took the stand, preached twice, and conducted a fellowship meeting. We had a glorious time; believers shouted; sinners wept; the word was quick and powerful; the prayers of God's people were heard, and *two* precious souls stepped into the liberty of His dear children. Hallelujah! Thus was this Hall dedicated to the service of the Most High. At this time our baby Ebenezer Hamar was so very sick we did not expect he would recover; yet Mrs. Acornley's own trouble did not prevent her from sympathizing with others in distressing circumstances. Writing to her mother-in-law, she says:—" I am in great trouble just now. I do not think dear baby will live. I have scarcely had any rest day or night for three weeks. I cannot tell you more now. . . . . . The people are exceedingly kind, we want for no sympathy or respect. . .

"Cousin Jane Eleanor's husband went out West two months ago. She is still in Cornwall. He has died, and is buried in a strange land, without a friend to close his eyes. Poor girl, she is in deep trouble. I feel for her very much." As the reader will here see by the foregoing extract, an allusion is made to the death of her cousin's husband (Mr. George) while at Treasure City, Nevada. He died and was buried among strangers, having been but a few weeks in the country. Mrs. Acornley wrote the young widow a letter of condolence; and as we have not the letter at hand, the following extract from the reply she received will indicate the tenor of her epistle:

"St. Day, Cornwall,
January 25th, 1872.

" My dear cousins:

"I need hardly tell you that your kind, though short, letter was to me very welcome. If anybody ever needed sympathy, I think it is myself. I pray, my dear, that such a trial as mine may never befall you; for no one can imagine what it is like except those who have passed through the same. My Bible tells me that 'whom the Lord loveth he chasteneth,' therefore I do strive to bow meekly to the rod, believing that He, who is too wise to err, knows best what is good for me, and if he did not love me I should not be so chastened. But oh, it is very hard to feel submissive to the divine will, but I do pray for grace to make me so. Pray for me, my dear cousins, both of you; I earnestly ask your interest at the throne of grace; please remember me. I should very much like to see you, I have a great deal to say to you, but I feel as if I cannot write it, at least not just now, and *I am afraid I shall never see you again in this world,* you are so very, very far away. . . . . . I have one true friend above, and to Him I look for all my help. I feel assured that if I trust in Him and do my duty He will be what He has promised, the 'Husband of the widow and the Father of the fatherless.' . . . . . I see from your address you have again changed residences. I should be glad to know, if it is not asking too much, what your prospects in life are? Has your dear husband entered the ministry? I almost conclude he has from the tone of your letter, though you do not positively say so. . . . . . I would ask you to kindly write to me very often, your letters will do me good, and give me a little consolation. . . . . . Please let me have a reply very soon, for I shall be anxiously waiting for it. And now, with kindest love to you both, believe me,

"Yours, most affectionately,

"JANE ELEANOR GEORGE.

"Kiss the babies for me."

Our Annual Conference, which met in Tamaqua on the 1st of May, stationed us for Plymouth Circuit along with brother W. B. Beach. We resided at Hughestown, a little village about a mile from the town of Pittston, Luzerne County. Pittston is built on the banks of the river Susquehanna, in the beautiful valley of Wyoming. The surrounding scenery is indeed lovely. By some, this valley is said to be the garden of Pennsylvania.

"On Susquehanna's side, fair Wyoming!
 .   .   .   .   .
Sweet land! may I thy lost delight recall."
Campbell.

"Oh! not the visioned poet in his dreams,
When silvery clouds float through the 'wildered brain,
When every sight so lovely, wild and grand,
Astonishes, enraptures, elevates—
When fancy, at a glance, combines
The wond'rous and the beautiful,—
So bright, so fair, so mild a scene,
Hath ever yet beheld."
Shelley.

It is claimed that the German Missionary, Count Zinzendorf, was the first white man who ever beheld the beauties of this romantic section of country. In the year 1742 he sought, in the wilds of the forest, to proclaim the glad tidings of salvation to the untutored savage. Fierce and prolonged wars have taken place in this valley, and the blood of white man and red man has mingled in mortal strife. During those border wars atrocious crimes were perpetrated, and wrongs committed both on white man and Indian.

> "Nature hath made thee lovelier than the power
> Even of Campbell's pen hath pictured; he
> Had woven, had he gazed one sunny hour
> Upon thy winding vale, its scenery,
> With more of truth, and made each rock and tree
> Known like old friends, and greeted from afar;
> And there are tales of sad reality
> In the dark legions of thy border war,
> With woes of deeper tint than his own Gertrude's are."
> *Halleck.*

Clark, the historian, says, when speaking of " Wyoming's classic vale," " Its own intrinsic loveliness has been the theme of poet and tourist since the day when enraptured eyes first beheld it. Its historical incidents have been breathed over the firesides of the entire American nation. Its sudden and giant-like growth has drawn to it the wonder and applause of the world, while its seemingly exhaustless supply of mineral wealth, challenges the astonishment of the old world, that but a century ago had never dreamed of this *El Dorado* in the forests of America."

A great change has now come over the entire face of the country. Where once the wild man ran, and the crack of the huntsman's rifle was heard; now the evidences of civilization appear on every hand. How marked the change!

The impression seems to prevail in the minds of some people, that in the coal section of these Pennsylvania mountains there is nothing but dense moral darkness, barbarous rudeness, and savage ferocity. This, however, we are proud to say, is only so to a very limited extent; although we admit that much that is sinful and sad exists among these mountains; yet we must say that those persons who entertain the views we have alluded to, have only seen the dark side, or heard exaggerated statements, and have thus formed unjust conclusions concerning these "hardy sons of toil."

Miners, as a class, have their besetments and vices, it is true; nor would it be untrue to say that numbers of them are rough in appearance and deportment; yet beneath that rough exterior are often found generous sentiments, refined feelings, manly qualities, warm hearts and holy lives. Religion flourishes to a considerable extent among these mountains. There are spots which are illuminated with brilliant and glorious rays of moral sunshine; and in those spots there are heads as clear, intellects as quick, reputations as pure, and characters as unstained as can be found under more favorable circumstances in any city, town, or village from the Atlantic to the Pacific coast. To these "hardy sons" we are indebted for many of the comforts we enjoy. Some poet has sung—

"Before the miner pierced the field,
The soldier had no sword to wield;
To sailors Neptune would not yield
Old ocean, like a parchment sealed.

The rail-car had not kept the rail,
Nor steamships sped without a sail;
The lightnings had not told their tale
From northern hill to southern vale."

Again the same poet has sung—

> "The sailor's life has its round of charms,
> The storm and chase with their wild alarms;
> And he sings as the boatswain pipes to arms.
> 'Ho! ho! for the sea with its mystic charms.'
>
> The soldier fights for a scanty hire,
> Yet pants for the strife and the battle's fire;
> As he to the rampart's heights aspires
> Sings—'ho! for the strife and the battle's fire.'
>
> The farmer treads o'er his furrowed land,
> And scatters seed with his careful hand,
> And sings as he twists his shining bands,
> 'Ho! ho! for hearty harvest hands.'
>
> The miner pants for no gory goal;
> In vain to him may the battle roll;
> Yet his manly heart and his fearless soul
> Sings —'ho! success to the gleaming coal.'
>
> We dig by day, and we dig by night,
> For the iron ore and the anthracite—
> For the ore so gray, and the coal so bright;
> Sing ho! for the ore and the anthracite."

Mrs. Acornley was eminently fitted for the office of minister's wife. Solomon says, "A virtuous woman is a crown to her husband." "Her price is far above rubies. The heart of her husband doth safely trust in her." "She will do him good, and not evil, all the days of her life." "Every pastor stands in need of encouragement, of cheerfulness, of peace in his own home, to enable him to bear what life brings with it, and still to preserve the power of working for the benefit of mankind." And a good wife is not only a benefit to him personally, but is certainly an acquisition to any community. She helps the pastor, makes for him a pleasant home, increases the social feeling between him and his people, and is a blessing to them in many ways. The fundamental qualities which every true minister's wife ought to possess are good common sense, mental culture, and sincere piety—which includes faith, love, courage, zeal, meekness, patience, and humility. Of course there will not be perfection in all, or any one of these graces, neither is it claimed for the subject of this memoir; mistakes she did make at times, but in all she conscientiously endeavored to discharge her duties as they rose. There are many unthinking people in our churches who expect a good minister's wife to be found, like some garments, a complete fit; they expect her to be as the *Baptist Magazine* says, "Warranted never to have headache or neuralgia; she should have nerves of wire and sinews of iron; she should never be tired or sleepy, and should be everybody's cheerful drudge; she should be cheerful, intellectual, pious and domesticated; should be pleased with everybody and everything, and never desire any reward beyond the satisfaction of having done her own duty, and other people's too." And then, if she does not come up to these requirements, they are ready to grumble and find fault. This ought not so to be, for it is the training *in* the sphere that qualifies her *for* it, though some have more native congeniality to the station than others. The true minister's wife, while she is endeavoring, as in the sight of her heavenly Master, to do her duty,

> "She knows
> Herself the mark of scrutinizing eyes,
> And curious observations. Apt remarks
> Are ventured, subtle questions asked, to prove
> And fathom her opinions."

And, although in her experience she finds that "there are shadows as well as lights, clouds as well as sunshine, thorns as well as roses, but much happiness after all," she realizes that—

> "Duty is a prickly shrub, but its flower will be happiness and glory."

In household affairs Mrs. Acornley displayed much good taste. When, like many others not in affluent circumstances, she had not furniture sufficient for use and convenience, she stayed not to murmer or repine, but carefully adorned her home with all the little articles of beauty or value which kind friends had given her. She was very fond of choice flowers and beautiful leaves, and when she wrote to her various friends, would often insert a leaf, or a dried flower in the envelope. Writing to her father, who at that time resided in the state of Minnesota, she says:—"Those leaves you enclosed were really beautiful. I have not lost my taste for flowers, trees and ferns; though I have grown from a child to a woman. I have still that childish will to watch over a few flowers with tender care, and I love to examine beautiful leaves." She would have endorsed every sentiment contained in the following lines, by the Countess of Blessington:

> "Flowers are the bright remembrancers of youth;
> They waft us back, with their bland odorous breath,
> The joyous hours that only young life knows,
> Ere we have learnt that this fair earth hides graves.
> They bring the cheek that's mouldering in the dust
> Again before us, tinged with health's own rose;
> They bring the voices we shall hear no more,
> Whose tones were sweetest music to our ears;
> They bring the hopes that faded one by one,
> 'Till nought was left to light our path but faith,
> That we too, like the flowers, should spring to life,
> But not, like them, again e'er fade or die."

And then, with Bernard Barton, she might have said

> "If such the soothing precepts taught by you,
> Beautiful blossoms! well may ye appear
> As silent preachers in the Christian's view."

Her house was the abode of affection, peace, comfort and joy; and notwithstanding many privations, it might be said of her home and family, that

> "There each soul with heavenly hope is blest,
> And every thought of strife is hushed to rest.
> There sweet affection its mild radiance throws,
> And bids each heart in mutual love repose.
>
> O, they have comforts that all griefs defy,
> And joys that wealth and greatness cannot buy,
> Treasures laid up in realms of endless day,
> A kingdom that shall never pass away;

> And e'en on earth to them the seal is given,
> Of their eternal heritage in Heaven.
> 'Tis this which to that lowly cottage brings
> Such peace, from this their heartfelt gladness springs.
> This sheds a halo round each changing scene,
> And gilds earth's desert waste with joys serene."

Affliction and bereavement, however, soon entered that peaceful home. Our little one, Ebenezer Hamar, was taken away to mingle with that countless multitude of children "around the throne of God in heaven." The tender tiny rose, "fair and beautiful as a truant one from Eden, planted by some seraph's hand," was "nipped in the bud."

> "There's not a flock, however watched and tended,
> But one dead lamb is there;
> There's not a household, howsoe'er defended,
> But has one vacant chair."

This was a sore trial. The more sickly and troublesome children are, the closer they seem to twine themselves round a good mother's heart, and consequently, the harder it is to part with them. This dear child was born amidst distressing circumstances and anxious cares; nevertheless, with many tears and many prayers, he was laid on God's altar, and in Jesus' arms, and consecrated to the Most High. And when his short probation was ended, as she gazed on his little pale face, as he lay cold and still in death, although her heart seemed well nigh with anguish riven, she did not sorrow as one without hope, but was enabled to see the hand of her beneficent

Lord, and could say from her heart, "The Lord gave and the Lord hath taken away, blessed be the name of the Lord." She was consoled with the thought that he was only gone a little ahead; that the good Lord had only plucked her *rose-bud*, that it might open into flower in the garden of God.

When this occurred her sorrow was augmented by a feeling of loneliness, having been but a few weeks on this station, and consequently being among strangers. However, the friends were very kind, and our babe was laid in his little grave in "sure and certain hope of the resurrection to eternal life," Rev. W. B. Beach officiating. The following paper, written about this time, will illustrate her feelings, and give an idea of the devotion which pervaded her mind under these afflictive circumstances:

"Through the various changing scenes of this (my) life, I have been made fully to realize that beautiful passage, 'I have never seen the righteous forsaken, nor his seed begging bread.' What confidence seems placed in those few words; what comfort the poor Christian may take if he trusts; what a holy feeling may pervade his whole frame, his whole actions, words and thoughts. Yea, 'though thy father and thy mother forsake thee, the Lord will take thee up.' Then why should I, a poor weak worm of the earth, yet an heir of heaven; I, an erring daughter of Eve, yet a child of God; I, unworthy and polluted, yet a sinner saved by grace; why should I faint, why should I despond or feel sad? my Father knows my fears; He can defend me; He knows my weakness, He can protect and strengthen me. 'Praise the Lord, O my soul, and forget not all his benefits.' Truly I can say and feel that 'Hitherto the Lord hath helped me.' The removal of our darling Ebenezer is, I trust, a blessing in disguise. I do feel that through it my heart has been purified. My Father thought the flower or bud had bloomed long enough down here, so now it blooms in the garden of paradise. I may not feel very well in body, but my soul is on full stretch for the kingdom. This morning we went to church—very few present*—yet though cast down, not forsaken, we each had a blessing,

> 'The Lord came down our souls to greet,
> While glory crown'd the mercy seat.'

This afternoon I went to school, just at time, sent for the keys and started; addressed the scholars on the *Deluge;* had a very interesting season. Went to church at 6 o'clock; Bro. P— started the service; we had a very good congregation after all, and truly we felt cheered. Bro. P— spoke from the words, 'Let not your heart be troubled,' &c. And indeed why need we? for if faithful unto death, the promise

---

* The reason of so few being present was owing to the fact of nearly all the society having removed out West; a number went to Ohltown, Ohio, and formed a society which is now the head of a station.

is, a robe of righteousness; a crown of glory; a palm of victory; and we shall drink of the river of life; eat of the tree in the midst of the garden; we shall hunger no more; nor thirst any more; and God, *even our God* (how beautiful! how sublime!) shall wipe all tears from our eyes. A dear sister of the M. E. Church spoke, and truly the Lord was in our midst; we all felt good. I am sure, I think we frightened old Satan clear away."

A. R. A.

Her own health was very feeble at this time, hence she wrote as follows to her mother-in-law:

August 14th, 1872.

"My beloved mother,

"Do not think me negligent or thoughtless for not writing to you sooner. My mind is quite upset, and I have not had any desire, or heart, to write. I am not well at all, and unless there is a great change speedily I shall be soaring away. I seem to grow weaker each day. If I do go away, I would like our dear, only boy, Benjamin Richard, to be under his dear grandmama's care, *please remember*. He is a dear child." . . . . .

After speaking of the affection of her eldest child for his little brother, who was gone, she continues: "I do not mourn for my child, wishing him to return, dear mother, but only a mother who has lost or parted with a dear one, knows my feelings, or can truly sympathize with me. Our darling was always sickly and weak; and had it pleased the Lord to spare his life, I think he would never have been a strong man. . . . . . . The Lord lent him to us a little time, and now He hath need of him. I cannot repine, dear mother. He was indeed a lovely flower; every one used to say, 'what a beautiful child.' . . . . . I seem now to have a tie that should bind me to this land, and likewise another link to bind me to the glory land. Pray for us, dear mother, that we may be kept steadfast. I do sincerely wish that you and dear Fred, and Sam, and Polly were all here. . . . . . If you come, I shall come to live with you, dear mother, to get well again. I need a gentle hand to take care of me, for my mind seems shattered; I dont know why. I do not repine. . . . . . May God bless you, dear mother, and the children.

"Your affectionate daughter,
"AGNES REBECCA ACORNLEY.

She had purposed, had circumstances permitted, visiting her native land, England. But in this she was doomed to disappointment; still she did not repine. Writing to her husband's mother, at different times, she says: "Disappointments await us at all times; you and I are permitted to receive another; before I name it you know what it is. I thought that before now—in this month—I should have had the unspeakable pleasure of taking a good cup of tea *with you*. But circumstances alter cases sometimes." Speaking of the division of the circuit, she says: "We have *eight* preaching places; it will be hard work; the local help is insufficient, but I trust, with God's blessing, we shall do wonders: already the cloud seems to be breaking. We have managed to build a little church since we came on the circuit." Again, " now do try to write, if only a line or two, or let brother Sam; we have been very anxious to hear how brother Fred is; it seems so very strange no one writes. You know we are away, but you have no idea how we prize a line, or a paper. Brother William has been real good to send us so many P. M's and B. W's (Primitive Methodists and British Workman.) I hope he will continue, for they are so valuable; they please and interest us more than one pennyworth. We have only had one letter from him since our birdie flew away; but he has got other cares of a domestic nature, and we excuse him. But you know my feelings, you can imagine how very lonely we are sometimes. If we have things cross our path, to try our faith, or Christian fortitude, we have *not one* of our relatives to whom we can tell our trouble or relieve our mind. Those at home can fly to you in person, and you can advise and sympathize with them there and then; but we are here, and when cast down, no one of our own to sympathize or advise. We cannot write what we could tell you. Do write and let us know how you all are." Again, she says: "Our missionary meetings are just over; they have proved a real success, seeing they are the first ever held by our people up in this region. We hope to realize $75.00 by the effort. We are still short of our salary, but we have never wanted for provisions. Only money is short, and we hope to obtain that. Our circuit is a very hard one; the roads are rough to travel, the weather is most severe. John is ofttimes weary in the work, but not of the work. I pray he may never be. He is so much away from home he has not time enough for study. I do not know how he manages at all. It is not all pleasure to be a minister or a minister's wife; there is every disposition to watch, and form yourself to. But amid all our discouragements we have a very great deal to be thankful for. Our societies have suffered greatly from removals. A very great many have gone west on account of work, trade in general about here being so bad; this makes our money matters bad, and our societies weak."

Speaking of her approaching sickness, she says: "I feel very sad over it somehow, though I ought, and *do* try to leave it in the hands of my heavenly Father. I feel as if I shall not see over it; the cold is intense; many are dying round here. I hope you will pray for me. I do wish you were here, and then all would go right, I know. If anything happens to me, I hope you will take our Benjamin Richard, and may the Lord bless you."

God, however, was better to her than all her fears. He kindly brought her through the furnace of affliction, and made her the living mother of a living child. Ought not feelings of gratitude to fill the hearts of Christian parents for God's great goodness to them at these times. So it was with the subject of this memoir; joyous emotions, sunny hopes, tender attachment, and unfeigned gratitude filled her heart, and often found expression on her tongue. It was to her a

> "Delightful task! to rear the tender thought,
> To teach the young idea how to shoot,
> To pour the fresh instruction o'er the mind,
> To breathe the enlivening spirit, and to fix
> The generous purpose in the glowing breast."

And often have we felt

> "Our heart grow softer as we gazed upon
>   That youthful mother, as she soothed to rest,
> With a low song, her loved and cherished one,
>   The bud of promise on her gentle breast;
> For 'tis a sight that angel ones above
>   May stoop to gaze on from their bowers of bliss,
> When Innocence upon the breast of Love
>   Is cradled, in a sinful world like this."

In a letter to her father, referring to one of her children, she says: "I pray he may be spared to be an ornament to the church, a pillar to build her up, and a *bright* light to go out no more forever. I want and pray that he may do the work we have left undone."

About this time the Rev. B. Whillock, Mrs. Acornley's father, met with a very serious accident, while driving in a cutter one Sunday to perform the services at a funeral. The horse ran away, the cutter upset, and he was thrown over on the ice. His collar bone was broken, and he was otherwise injured in different parts of the body. In reply to a letter of her sister's, informing her of this misfortune, she wrote,

"My dear sister Fanny,

"I was really very glad to hear from you yesterday, though sorry to hear of father's misfortune. You never spoke one word of your mother. I consider that an oversight. I wish to know of all your welfare. Do not fail to keep me posted. I am sorry you suffer with the headache. I trust you will never suffer as I do. I fall insensible sometimes with the excessive weakness; my sight goes, and through my temples one convulsive throb, and I am gone. I am alone most of the time. It is not altogether safe; though when I feel to go blind, I lie down on the sofa a few minutes, with my eyes closed, and so put it off. For several years I have suffered severely with pain in the head, and whatever I try does not seem to do me much good. . . . . .

I hope you will write often and let me know how you each are. Now do not fail, as I shall be very anxious; meanwhile accept my warmest love as a sister.
"Agnes Rebecca."

To her father she wrote as follows:

February, 1873.
" My dear father,

"I am sure I need not tell you how very deeply I sympathize with you in your great affliction. I have not words to express my sorrow or sympathy. I sincerely trust you may be speedily restored, though I am afraid never to your former strength. I had a forewarner of a something, and have been deeply and doubly anxious of late. I have still terrible misgivings. I trust nothing more serious will occur. My dear John never goes away from home but something whispers, will he return to me again safe? I try to leave these things in the hands of my heavenly Father. Our prayer daily arises from the family altar for you, and the welfare, temporally and spiritually, of each of you.

"You must not think it strange I do not write to you more often. I have never felt like writing or sitting still long enough to write since our birdie flew away *eight* months ago; our house has never seemed the same. But the flower blooms in a more congenial and heavenly atmosphere, and soon we will smell the fragrance, if faithful unto the end. I need not ask if you suffer pain, I am sure you must. Do write often and let us know how you are—or rather Fanny. I was very glad indeed to see her handwriting. I hope she will not fail to let us see it often. . . . . . We are very anxious. I hope, through mercy, you will soon recover; and that in this affliction you may feel the hand of God resting upon you in love. May you feel that though He has afflicted you, yet not forsaken you. In His providence He has ordered it so. May He ever bless you, and keep you *faithful*, is the prayer, daily, of your fond daughter,

"Agnes Rebecca Acornley."

February, 1873.

Referring to the difficulties connected with the erection of several churches on this station—Wilkes-Barre and Pittston—and also to the continued kindness of her numerous friends, in a letter to her sister she says: "We are somewhat short of our salary, but if we succeed in building and getting the churches in easy circumstances, I can bear the loss better, though we need money as much as most people. Our members are pretty kind. I believe we have the respect of all. . . . . . Do you still like your circuit? you seem to be making yourself useful. I hope you will still try to live, and let people *feel* and *know* that you live. We are accountable beings, and according as we have shall it be required again.

May the Lord bless you, my dear, is the prayer of your affectionate sister."

Again, to her father, she writes: "We have much to be thankful for. I feel thankful to the people, but I feel doubly thankful that the Lord has inclined their hearts toward us; I can safely say we have not one opponent or enemy on the circuit. We try to do our duty as becomes the gospel; I think if there is a man on the face of the earth that tries to act consistent and charitable, working the doctrine of the gospel, and with an eye single to God's glory, it is my dear husband. I pray that the God of Jacob may defend and uphold him; strengthen him in body for the work, fire his heart, and give him seals to his ministry and souls for his hire."

The friends were ready to seize every opportunity of showing their kindness, hence it was determined to celebrate our "Wooden Wedding." To those who are unacquainted with this custom, we may remark, that it is usual to celebrate weddings in this manner, when the friends of the parties bring presents in character with the occasion. For instance, at a "Wooden Wedding" the guests are expected to bring some article of that material. At a "Silver Wedding" something of silver, and so forth, through the list of anniversaries. We may also observe that the *fifth* anniversary is "Wooden," the *tenth* is "Tin," the *fifteenth* is "Crystal," the *twenty-fifth* is "Silver," and the *fiftieth* is "Golden."

On the evening of the *fifth* anniversary of our marriage—December 17th, 1873, a number of friends gathered and enjoyed a cup of tea together at the parsonage, each one bringing an expression of their good-will in the shape of a present of something or other; the evening was then profitably and pleasantly spent in singing and conversation. The *Pittston Gazette*, of the next week, contained the following reference to it:—

"HYMENIAL.

"*Wooden Wedding.*—On the evening of the 17th, the friends of the Rev. John H. and Mrs. Acornley, Primitive Methodist minister at Plains, Pa., gathered at the parsonage to celebrate their ' Wooden Wedding.' The evening was very pleasantly spent in ministering to the necessities of the ' inner man,' &c. Some excellent pieces were rendered by an amateur choir. Numerous presents of useful articles were furnished by the guests, and expressions of good will indulged in; and hopes were entertained that the reverend gentleman and his lady might be spared many years, enjoy a long life of happiness and usefulness here, and finally spend an eternity in Heaven."

After having spent two years on this station, we were removed to Morris Run, Tioga County, in the northern part of the State of Pennsylvania. But previous to our removal Dr. Shive, Sister Moore and Bro. James Hilburt (a young man of great promise, who, while rising quickly from bed a day or two afterwards, fell, and striking his neck on the top of a broken lamp globe, which stood on a chair by his bed side, severed his jugular vein, the blood flowed profusely, and he died in a few minutes,) were the promoters of an agreeable surprise in the shape of drygoods, groceries, and a small sum of money. Thus the last act of this young man in connection with the church of Christ was an act of kindness towards his minister and family. A number of ladies in Pleasant Valley, got together and made a handsome quilt, on which was inscribed, in the centre of each block, the names of the donors, and sent in to Mrs. Acornley as an expression of their respect and esteem. This she carefully treasured as long as she lived. These are not a tithe of the kind manifestations of affection which she received; and the friends she made while on this station lived in her affections as long as life lasted.

"Friendship! mysterious cement of the soul!
Sweet'ner of life, and solder of society,
I owe thee much! thou hast deserved of me
Far, far beyond what I can ever pay."

John L. Sexton, Jr., Esq., in his account of Morris Run, says: " Morris Run, located on a mountain stream bearing the same name, situated four miles east of Blossburg, in the township of Hamilton, in Tioga County, is one of the great mining towns in the semi-bituminous coal-fields of northern Pennsylvania. About twenty-two years ago, these mines were opened by the Tioga Improvement Company." Since then they have passed through various hands, until now they are owned and worked by the Morris Run Coal Mining Company, W. S. Nearing, Esq., agent. Improvements have continually been made, and the capacity of the mines increased, so that now they are enabled to produce 2,500 tons per day. The total shipment of coal for the year ending Jan. 1st, 1874, reached the vast sum of 357,384 tons. This was exclusive of their home and other sales. About eight hundred men are employed; of these 450 are miners, and about 350 are connected with other branches of the work. The town contains about 2,500 inhabitants, who dwell in 356 houses. There is but one store, which is owned by the company; Major Anderson being the principal agent. There are three churches in Morris Run, viz., Welsh Baptist, Welsh Congregational, and Primitive Methodist. These are neat structures, surmounted by tall spires, intimating to a stranger the moment he enters the town, that the spiritual welfare of the inhabitants is not neglected.

In the evening of the day we arrived on our new station a number of friends gathered at the parsonage to accord us a hearty welcome. Each one brought something to please the palate, and appease the cravings of the stomach. The tables were laden, and every one seemed to enjoy a social cup of that which "cheers but not inebriates." After which words of welcome and good will were freely indulged in, and hopes expressed that the newly formed associations might have God's blessing, and that during the coming year the work of the Lord might prosper, sinners be saved, and God's name be glorified.

In a short time after her arrival in Morris Run, Mrs. Acornley was seized with another attack of sickness, this time accompanied with inflammation in the eyes, rendering her almost blind. While suffering intense pain one day, her children playing around until they were tired, and she being unable to attend to their wants, the little one became uneasy and cross; this made her feel keenly her affliction, and calling him to her, she began to soothe and comfort him; at the same time tears coursing down her face. Her eldest child—a little over four years old at this time—observing his mother weeping, attempted to console her, saying, "Don't cry ma! don't cry! I try and find out where the Lord lives, and I go and fetch him, don't cry ma! He 'll make *mud* to make you well. If He don't put it on your eyes, I will, don't cry ma! you be better." And placing his little hand on her face, the dear child, thus attempted in his way to comfort her, nor was it in vain. She had related to her child the story of Christ healing the blind man, and now that lesson, replete with force and beauty, had returned to her own soul rich and mellow with instruction and consolation. A fresh flood of tears burst forth, and her heart welled up with gratitude and love to her heavenly Father who had thus made her child the means of comforting her soul. Blessed be God, "Out of the mouth of babes and sucklings He has ordained strength." The loss of her little one was a subject which still occupied her mind considerably. Writing to her sister, she says, "It is two years to-day since we laid our dear little rose-bud down to sleep, until the sound of the trumpet. What a very pleasant two years he must have spent up there! don't you think?" referring to her new home and friends, she says, "I do not like this part of the country so well as our former residence, but *I like the people, I feel I shall be real happy with them.*" Mrs. Acornley received the following letter from a lady belonging to the M. E. Church, but who had frequently attended our church at Wilkes-Barre, and for whom she had formed a sincere attachment.

"Wilkes-Barre, Oct. 14th, 1874.
" Mrs. Acornley,
" Dear sister :

" Your kind epistle came safely to hand. I was sorry to hear that you had been sick. Mr. Acornley not well, and the little boy ailing.

" I have sincere sympathy for a preacher's wife going to a strange place, but as a *mother* I can enter into her feelings, knowing well the anxious watchings over the little ones—and the *sorrow* over the precious ones, as the light has gone out of the bright eyes *for-*

ever, and the active little limbs grown strangely still. And I know too what it is to go to a strange place and leave the little *mounds* of earth so dear to us in the *far away*.

"I hope by this time that you are much better, as well as your husband and the little ones. I hope also that you may find in your new home, some congenial *spirit* who *will* cheer and comfort you in those hours which come to *all*, when the hearty counsel of a kind friend is grateful and helpful. . . . . .

"I was at your church last Sunday evening for the first time since you left, there was a good congregation. . . . . .

"My kind regards to your husband, and I trust you may *both* be *cheered* by seeing the *Master's* work prospering under your labors. However if you do not *see* the results, you *know* that it will not be *vain*, but the *rewards are sure*.

"Remember at a throne of grace

"Your unworthy sister,

"R. G. MITCHELL."

The friends in Morris Run were exceedingly kind; and sought in every way in their power to compensate for the dullness of times. They seemed determined that hard weather and dull times should not interfere with the comfort of their minister or his family; and hence "Pound Parties," "Peck Parties," and pleasant "Surprises" in many ways, visited the parsonage on various occasions. The *Blossburg Register* contained the following paragraph in reference to one of them.

"*Morris Run.*—On Wednesday evening, Dec. 9th, 1874, another band of crusaders started out in Morris Run, and besieged the house of Rev. John H. Acornley (Primitive Methodist Minister). The inmates were surprised, and consequently soon brought to surrender. The besiegers took possession of the premises, when it was discovered that each of the attacking party was armed with bags of potatoes, beets, apples, onions, and other weapons too numerous to mention. Having gained admission, the crusaders laid down their weapons, hostilities ceased, their arms were stacked, and peace and good will were soon manifest between the late apparent belligerents.

"Mr. Acornley and his wife were at a loss to give expression to their feelings at this manifestation of affection ; their prayer, however, is that God may bless every one of the ' Peck Party' who came to see them on Wednesday evening of last week."

Her intercourse with those who were not members of the church was of an affectionate and Christian character; and in order further to illustrate the affection and esteem in which she was held by both members of the church and congregation, we give the following incident: One evening, not being very well, she thought not to go to the Monday evening prayer-meeting, which was usually held at the house of some member or friend. On this occasion, however, when it was found that she did not purpose to come, several of the ladies started out to the parsonage; told her she must come, as they wanted to see her there. She came, wondering what made them so anxious. The meeting was indeed a blessed season. At its close, one of the brethren, W. C. Jenkins, rose to his feet and remarked that "godliness was profitable unto all things, having the promise of the *life that now is*, as well as of that which is to come; that those who live to God, and trust in him, shall be blessed with things *temporal*, as well as things spiritual, he was glad to see that they were unlike some societies who were always finding fault, and complaining about their minister's wife. Some minister's wives, he remarked, if they happened to have a little taste in dress, if they could trim up an old bonnet or hat, in order to make it last another season; or if they could turn an old cloak, to save purchasing a new one out of their scanty income, were sure to be accused of being proud and arrogant, above their station, or something of that sort. But he was pleased to find that it was not so in Morris Run; but so far from that, their minister's wife was loved and appreciated by the sisters in the church, and also by the ladies of the congregation. In proof of which, he had great pleasure in presenting to Mrs. Acornley, in the name and in behalf of the ladies, a small token of their respect and esteem." He then proceeded to present

Mrs. Acornley with a *tea-pot;* *half dozen tea spoons;* *and a beautiful quilt, the work of the ladies' own hands.* She was so overcome with the surprise that she could not give full expression to her feelings. However, she returned thanks, as best she could, to the ladies and friends, for their great kindness, and prayed that God would bless the labors of her dear husband, and herself among them; and, finally, that all might find their way to the better land. It would be impossible to enumerate all the manifestations of affection which she received from the friends of Morris Run; we may, however, say, that Mr. W. S. Nearing, the company's agent, was especially kind.

While I was attending the Annual Conference at Shenandoah City, she wrote as follows:

"Morris Run, Tioga County, Pa.
"April 11th, 1875.

"My dear John:

"Last night I received two letters from you, and was glad. Several of the brethren were here as soon as the mail, to know the news. There is quite a talk for fear you are removed. I have been real sick all week. I have not been to church to-day. Bro. Cook preached last Sabbath night, he had 'Strait is the gate, &c.' He said the gate was so strait that it would not admit a ball room dress, nor a bottle of whiskey.

"Bro. Young preached in the morning, and the

sermon was certainly a draught from Horeb. I went to school in the afternoon. To-day I am missing all, my side is bad, and headache intense. . . . . .
I shall not expect you back this week, only keep me posted each day. I think they will manage at church. They are all anxious that you come back *well*. With love, and a wife's true affection, I am still,

"Ever yours,

"AGNES REBECCA ACORNLEY."

This, as far as we are aware, was the last letter she ever wrote. To her husband she was a *help-meet* indeed, and in the performance of his ministerial duties was a great comfort and a constant help. Her morality was of the purest kind. Her temperance principles and practice were very strict. As a daughter she was tender and respectful. As a wife she was exemplary and loving. As a mother she was affectionate and kind. As a friend she was faithful and true. As a Christian she was consistent and earnest. Her religion was of a practical character, and shone most brilliantly in her own home. She was anxious to be a worker for Jesus, was much interested in the Sabbath school, and delighted in religious exercises, such as singing and prayer. One of the hymns she was particularly fond of was the following :—

"No mortal eye that land hath seen.
Beyond, beyond death's river;
Its smiling valleys, hills so green,
Beyond, beyond the river.

Its shores are drawing nearer,
Its skies are growing clearer,
Each day it seemeth nearer,
    That land beyond the river.
      CHORUS.—We'll stand the storm,
        We'll stand the storm,
        Its rage is almost over;
        We'll anchor in the harbor soon,
        In the land beyond the river.

No cankering care, no mortal strife,
    Beyond, beyond the river;
But happy, never-ending life,
    Beyond, beyond the river.
Through the eternal hours,
God's love in heavenly showers,
Shall water faith's fair flowers,
    In the land beyond the river.
      CHORUS.—We'll stand, &c.

That glorious day will ne'er be done,
    Beyond, beyond the river;
When we've the crown and kingdom won,
    Beyond, beyond the river.
There is eternal pleasure,
And joys that none can measure,
For those who have their treasure,
    In the land beyond the river.
      CHORUS.—We'll stand, &c.

When shall we stand on Zion's hill?
    Beyond, beyond the river;
Where endless bliss our hearts shall fill,
    Beyond, beyond the river.
There angels bright are singing,
And golden harps are ringing,
We ne'er shall cease our singing,
    In the land beyond the river.
      CHORUS.—We'll stand, &c."

Another which she sung often during the last few

months of her earthly pilgrimage was the consecration hymn.

"My body, soul and spirit,
Jesus, I give to thee,
A consecrated offering,
Thine evermore to be.
CHORUS.—My all is on the altar,
I'm waiting for the fire.

O Jesus, mighty Saviour,
I trust in thy great name,
I look for thy salvation,
Thy promise now I claim.
My all is on the altar, &c.

O let the fire descending,
Just now upon my soul,
Consume my humble offering,
And cleanse and make me whole.
My all is on the altar, &c.

I'm thine, O blessed Jesus,
Washed by thy precious blood,
Now seal me by Thy Spirit,
A sacrifice to God.
My all is on the altar, &c."

CHAPTER VI.

SICKNESS AND DEATH.

"Happy the spirit released from its clay;
Happy the soul that goes bounding away,
Singing, as upward it hastes to the skies,
Victory! Victory! homeward I rise.
Many the toils it has passed through below,
Many the seasons of trial and woe;
Many the doubtings it never should sing.
Victory! Victory! thus on the wing."

FOR several weeks previous to our Fourth of July celebration Mrs. Acornley had been so unwell that she was unable to leave the house. But so great was her anxiety to see the children, that with the assistance of several friends she reached the pic-nic grounds, remained there during the day, and appeared to enjoy herself immensely. On the 9th of July she was safely delivered of a fine male child. For several weeks she progressed very favorably and gathered strength. On Sunday, August 22d, she attended church in the evening and offered her child to God in the holy ordinance of baptism; Rev. F. T. Evans, Welsh Congregational minister, officiating.

On Tuesday, the 24th, she attended the funeral

service of our own next door neighbor's baby—Mr. Thos. Davis—in their own house; after which she went to visit the family of Mr. W. R. Gilmour, returning home in the evening. This was the last time she was out of doors. The next day she was very sick, which resulted in a severe attack of inflammation. The friends were very kind, and doctors very attentive. She, however, grew gradually worse. To her husband, who had just returned from his appointment at *Arnot*, on Sunday evening, August 29, she said: "O my dear, I feel assured I shall never recover, but this has been a blessed day to my soul." And then she went on to relate what sweet seasons of communion with God she had enjoyed during the day. This was the last conversation we had with her of any length. She suffered greatly during her affliction; her reason at times forsook her; and she was deprived of the power of speech, so that to hold intelligent conversation with her was almost an impossibility. It was sometimes really distressing to witness her struggle to say something; and it was with great difficulty that her attendants caught a word, or a disconnected sentence.

> "Gentle sufferer raise thine eye
> To thy home beyond the sky;
> Though thy earthly way be clouded,
> In the mist of sorrow shrouded,
> Yet there is rest for thee,
> Perfect, pure felicity.
> In yon Heaven of joy and love,
> There shall be no pain above."

The day following she appeared to be much better, and the doctor again had hopes of her ultimate recovery; she called, however, for her sister; a telegram was sent for her at once; she then called for her father. Both of them finally arrived and ministered incessantly to her needs, until she took her flight from this transitory scene.

Her husband being taken sick about the same time as herself, the children were taken away, and kindly cared for by friends; consequently the house wore a gloomy aspect. She was often seized with spasmodic convulsions, which violently worked her arms, and sometimes her head. Then her body would be so perfectly rigid that it was impossible to place her in an upright position. Many hours of anxious watching and attention followed. The house was seldom free from visitors anxious to know how she was, or to render assistance if required. A correspondent of the *Blossburg Register* wrote at this time, " Rev. J. H. Acornley, pastor of the P. M. Church of Morris Run, has been quite ill, but is recovering. Mrs. Acornley, his wife, is dangerously sick, and but little if any hope is entertained of her recovery. Much sympathy is felt for the family, and many prayers are ascending daily in their behalf "

When her sister arrived she recognized her and expressed herself glad, as she never expected to see her again. A day or two afterwards her father— Mr. Whillock—knelt down by the side of her bed, and poured out his soul to God in prayer on her behalf. While he was thus occupied, she looked at him as though unconscious of what he was engaged in; then brightening up she said, "Praise the Lord!" when he finished she responded "Amen."

About eleven days before she died, as her sister was about to retire, she kissed her and said, "Pray for me," to which Fanny responded, "yes, I will pray for you," when she said again, "yes, pray for me, and be a good girl." This was the last time she appeared conscious of Fanny's presence. The day following she seemed to have a presentiment of her approaching dissolution, for after having her frail suffering frame gently attended to, she turned to the wall, and her attendants heard her feebly whisper, "Ten more days rolled up in these clothes, and then they will be taken away." On Sunday, September 12th, she fixed her eyes steadfastly above and said, "yes! Ebenezer," as though speaking to her lost baby. Then after a pause she tried to sing "Jesus lover of my soul," &c. but could not. She appeared almost choked with suffering. Her mouth and throat were in a sad condition. Her mind wandered, and she appeared to be talking incoherently to herself and to her dear little children who were so soon to be left motherless. It appeared hard for her to utter anything, and her speech was very difficult to understand. On the evening of Friday, the 10th, consciousness had seemed to forsake her, and from that time she took but little notice of anything or anybody around her. On the 15th, however, consciousness returned for a few minutes, and she struggled to say something, but not one word could be understood. Her sight was affected during the last few days, and in one of these brief intervals of consciousness she was asked if she knew one of the ladies who were standing in the room; she failed to recognize her, and shook her head—speech being entirely gone—intimating that the person was unknown to her; when told who it was she wept at the thought of not being able to recognize her friends. Had she been able to speak, she would doubtless have consoled herself and friends with the thought that in heaven

" We shall know each other."

A few days before she died, while several ladies were tenderly raising her, her body being quite rigid, she evidently thought they imagined her gone, for with a mighty effort she called out quite loud and distinctly, as they took hold of her, " I'm not dead yet! I'm not dead yet!" She lingered a few days more, suffering intensely—mortification had set in—and, notwithstanding all the efforts of friends, physicians and family, she passed away on the morning of the 21st September, 1875, in the 28th year of her age.

" We stand beside the Christian's dying bed,
And watch the life stream ebbing fast away;

> There is no terror there, we would not stay
> The struggling spirit in its heavenward track;
> Nor its bright view of endless bliss delay,
> Or to earth's sorrows call the ransomed back."

We have the full assurance that she has gone to be with Jesus. We derive this blessed confidence, not only from the whispered words which with difficulty we heard before her death, but from assurances given at the commencement of her affliction; and better still from the whole tenor of her deportment during the seven years of our married life. During those years we traveled the path of life together, and through trials and sorrows, afflictions and bereavements, her conduct was always such as becometh the gospel of our Lord Jesus Christ.

> "O, but death is bliss!
> I feel as certain looking on the face
> Of a dead sister, smiling from her shroud,
> That our sweet angel hath but changed her place,
> And passed to peace, as when, amid the crowd
> Of the mad city, I feel sure of rest
> Beyond the hills—a few hours further west."
> *T. W. Parsons.*

Our loss is indeed great, and our sorrow extreme, but though a great loss to her family and friends, it is an incomparable gain to her. Though we have lost our companion, and sharer of our joys and sorrows, she has gained companionship with the glorified in heaven, and will continue to share in the delights of the redeemed for ever and ever. Though her three dear little children have lost a kind and affectionate mother, and a wide gap has been left in our family circle, she has gone to swell the blessed family circle of heaven, and has gained a home in the beautiful mansions of her beneficent Father in glory.

May we be enabled to take our bleeding, broken hearts to Jesus, and pour out our whole souls to Him, for He, and He alone, knows how to succor and support his afflicted children in every time of need. "Lo!" says He, "I am with you alway, even to the end of the world." "When thou passest through the waters I will be with thee, and through the rivers they shall not overflow thee; when thou walkest through the fire thou shalt not be burned, neither shall the flame kindle upon thee."

> "Oh! shall we weep, as one by one, the dear, the best-beloved go,
> And we are left alone and sad, to miss and mourn them here below?
> Nay, they are safe, though we have pain, and we shall meet them soon again."

Not knowing of her death, her husband's brother William wrote as follows:

September 27th, 1875.

"My dear brother,

"Mother has to-day received your second letter in reference to your own and Agnes's illness. We are all deeply sorry to hear that you are situated thus.

"A fortnight has elapsed since we received the first letter, and it has been a time of great trouble and suspense to us. A fortnight has passed since you wrote your second, and I do hope most sincerely that by this time Agnes will be somewhat recovered; but as you say, however well she gets on, she will be a long time before she can attend to her household duties. We shall not forget to remember you at the throne of Divine grace, and to pray that God's blessing, 'which maketh rich and addeth no sorrow,' may rest upon you; and that this affliction may be sanctified to your good, and to our good as well.

"It greatly rejoices our hearts to know that you can claim the promises of God, and that you experience the blessedness of a simple trust in Him. Continue to look up, my dear brother; think much upon the 'exceeding great and precious promises' contained in God's Word, and depend upon it that that word is true; although affliction and sorrow are things we do not like, yet these are among the 'all things' 'that work together for good to them that love God.' 'No chastening for the present is joyous, but grievous, but afterward it yieldeth the peaceable fruit of righteousness to them that are exercised thereby.' 'The eternal God is thy refuge, and underneath are the everlasting arms.' This last was my text at Stubley last night, and is a passage which has many a time been a great comfort to me.

"Mother wishes to know what you think about her

coming to you; she could ill be spared here, that is certain. She wishes to have your advice on the matter, &c. I know very well that you would only be too glad to have her come. But you are there, and know more about the country than we do; would it be advisable? Hoping that matters have by this time taken a turn for the better, and that we shall very soon hear from you again,

"I remain,

"Your ever affectionate brother,

"W. H. ACORNLEY."

Before this letter was written Mrs. Acornley was gone to realms of light and glory; and her happy spirit was basking in the sunlight of her Redeemer's presence.

"Beyond life's toils and cares,
Its hopes and joys, its weariness and sorrow,
Its sleepless nights, its days of smiles and tears,"
(In the) "bright unending morrow."

The funeral took place on the 23d of September, 1875. Such was the esteem in which she was held that nearly every person in the town attended and followed her remains to their last resting place, thus evincing their respect for the deceased, and their sympathy for those who had been bereaved. In order to give every one an opportunity of attending the funeral; also, as a mark of respect and sympathy, Mr. W. S. Nearing, the company's agent, kindly stopped all the works that afternoon. The Railroad company generously furnished extra cars to convey the mournful cortege to the place of interment. The "Good Templars" organization—of which she was a member—attended in full regalia. The sisters of this order, as well as those connected with the I. O. of O. F., manifested great attention during all the time of her affliction.

Knowing her love for flowers, a large and beautiful wreath of the choicest kind was made by one of the friends, and placed upon the casket as it was being borne by six of the brethren.

> "How much of memory dwells amidst thy bloom,
> Rose! ever wearing beauty for thy dower?
> The bridal day, the festival, the tomb,
> Thou hast thy part in each, thou stateliest flower!
> Therefore, with thy soft breath come floating by
> A thousand images of love and grief,
> Dreams, filled with tokens of mortality,
> Deep thought of all things beautiful and brief."
>
> Mrs. Hemans.

This beautiful memento of affection was placed upon the grave, where, for months, it remained after it had withered, a sad "token of mortality," reminding the passer-by that

> "The brightest day sinks into night,
> The fairest bud is touched with blight,
> There is no rest in things of sight—
>   Oh, no! not here."

The funeral service was conducted by the Rev. D. Savage, assisted by the Rev. C. Jones, (Welsh Baptist.) The church was crowded with an attentive and sympathetic audience. Her mortal remains were interred in the Blossburg burial ground.

"The grass grows green upon the yielding sod,
In this calm spot by careless steps untrod;
And tears are flowing o'er thy lowly tomb,
And sorrow's eye in vain would pierce the gloom."

Here

"Sleeps the precious dust, whose earnest faith
And humble love are registered on high."

"It is a lowly tomb. No marble there
Or sculptor's art doth blazon forth high birth,
Or deeds of proud renown."

For

"'Tis not on marble, nor on the gilded page
To print thy worth—thy charity display!
For chronicles like these may in an age
Be lost, and in oblivion pass away."
Howcroft.

CHAPTER VII.

REMEMBRANCE AND CONDOLENCE.

"But who amongst us can at first God's purposes divine?
'(She) being dead yet speaketh,' and (her) memory to this day
Is living, though (her) quiet grave lies many a mile away."

LET the reader, at his or her leasure, read the wise man's incomparable description of a virtuous woman, for, says he, "Her price is far above rubies." "Favor is deceitful and beauty is vain; but a woman that feareth the Lord shall be praised. Give her of the fruit of her hands; and let her own works praise her in the gates."—Prov. xxxi., 10–31.

Many expressions of condolence and encouragement, both verbal and written, were received by her bereaved husband, which were a great help to him; feeling as he did, that he was not without the sympathy of his brethren in the ministry as well as that of his family and more immediate friends; and he was brought to sweetly realize with Mrs. Hemans that

"The gloomiest day hath gleams of light.
The darkest wave hath bright foam near it;
And twinkles through the darkest night
Some solitary star to cheer it.

> The gloomiest soul is not all gloom,
> The saddest heart is not all sadness;
> And sweetly o'er the darkest doom
> There shines some lingering gleam of gladness.
>
> Despair is never quite despair,
> Nor life nor death the future closes;
> And round the shadowy brow of care
> Will hope and fancy twine their roses."

And as he thought of the watchful providence of his beneficent Father in heaven, he looked up and tremblingly said:

> " Father, take my hand,
> And reaching down, lead to the crown
> Thy child."

And the answer sweetly came:

> " The way is dark, my child; but leads to light:
> I would not have thee always walk by sight.
> My dealings now thou can'st not understand;
> I meant it so; but I will take thy hand,
> And through the gloom, lead safely home
> My child."

Then was he brought fully to realize that his heavenly Father

> " 'Himself hath done it.' Yes, although severe
> May seem the stroke, and bitter be the cup,
> 'Tis His own hand that holds it, and I know
> He'll give me grace to drink it meekly up."

The Rev. D. Savage, the day previous to Mrs. Acornley's death wrote as follows:

"TAMAQUA, September 20th.
"Dear brother:

"Yours to hand; how deeply do I feel for you. 'Hope thou in God, for thou shalt yet praise him.' I do hope sister Acornley is better; I lift my heart to God on your behalf, and pray, for your sake and the dear children's, that she may be spared, if consistent with the will of God. If it is otherwise, anything I can do I will. Look up brother; behind a frowning providence God hides a smiling face. Tell sister A. from me—keep hold of the cross, trusting in the blood; Victory is certain! Land is ahead! The crown is shining! Jesus is waiting! His grace is certain victory! We will meet on the banks! and never say farewell.

"With love, yours in haste,
"D. SAVAGE."

On the day of the funeral the Rev. F. T. Evans—Welsh Congregational minister—being unable to attend, wrote as follows:

"BLOSSBURG, Tioga Co., Pa.
"Sept. 23d, 1875.
"Mr. Acornley,
"Dear brother:

"Please ask brother Savage—if you deem it proper—to make known the reason of my absence from the funeral of your dear and beloved wife, and my sister, Mrs. Acornley. I should like for him to do so for my sake as well as for the public at large. . . . . . My brother, I feel very sorry I could not be present. Trust to God whom you faithfully serve. 'Cast thy burden upon the Lord, he shall sustain thee.' He shall never suffer the righteous to be moved. My brother, take comfort in the Lord in your bereavement. . . . . . .

"Your sincere brother,
"F. T. Evans."

In an obituary sketch, which was published in *Our Messenger*, for January, 1876, the Rev. D. Savage says: "Bro. Acornley, in the year 1871, was called by our conference to the work of the ministry. The sacrifices he had to make were cheerfully borne by his companion. The burdens he has had to bear, peculiar to the work of the ministry, were made lighter by her sympathy. The genuineness of her piety, and the deep love she had for the cause, the members and friends of her husband's charges can bear testimony to. Her strong temperance principles will be understood, when it is remembered she was a faithful and earnest Good Templar."

At a regular meeting of Morris Run Lodge of Good Templars, No. 740, the following preamble and resolutions were adopted:

Whereas, It has pleased our heavenly Father to remove by death our beloved sister Agnes Rebecca

Acornley, thus severing the fraternal ties that so pleasantly existed in the past, and

Whereas, We regret with sadness her departure to that bourne from whence no traveler returns, be it therefore

Resolved: First, That while we recognize with reverence the will of our heavenly Father, we are filled with sorrow at the loss we have sustained, in one who by her generous, kind and genial disposition, won our love and highest respect, and who as a Good Templar, was ever found ready and willing to do her duty. And be it furthermore

Resolved: Second, That our charter be draped, and that the members wear a badge of mourning for thirty days; and that these resolutions be printed in the *Blossburg Register*, and a copy of the same be presented, with sympathy of the lodge, to our beloved brother and husband of the deceased.

" Upon the pallid marble brow,
 The auburn tresses lie.
 Her dark blue eyes are closed for aye,
 Beneath the autumn sky.

 The firm brave lips will speak no more,
 The words of truth and love,
 For hushed in joy, the spirit flies,
 To rest in realms above."

J. O. Chapman,	J. Bennett, L. D.,
N. M. Loper,	Fanny J. Wilson,
W. S. Rexford.	*Committee.*

Morris Run, Oct. 1st, 1875.

The Rev. Henry Wheeler—uncle of Mrs. Acornley—who is now superannuated and resides in Newport, Monmouthshire, writes:

"92 Dock Street, Newport, Mon.,
"Dec. 7, 1875.

" My dear Mr. Acornley,

" Your letter, informing us of the removal by death of your beloved wife, arrived here yesterday, for which I tender you best thanks.

" We were all of us anxious to be furnished with some particulars in reference to that event, and have had much pleasure in reading the particulars of her peaceful passage from hence to the glory land, and are happy for the blessed assurances that she is now 'Safe in the arms of Jesus'—safe for ever and ever, praise the God of our salvation, praise him for the blessed One who has overcome for us 'the sharpness of death,' and opened 'the kingdom of heaven to all believers.' 'Blessed are the dead which die in the Lord,' so 'saith the spirit,' and we have therefore no reason nor room for anxiety or doubt.

" We sincerely sympathize with you in your trouble, but you must not allow it to cast you down; try to bow with the most profound veneration whilst with faltering accent you utter the words of one of old, 'It is the Lord, let him do what seemeth him good.'

'He is His own interpreter,
And He will make it plain.'

"You must brace up your nerves, and look your difficulties full at once, and then cast your burden wholly on the Lord, and he shall sustain thee. If Agnes is dead, Jesus lives;—Jesus, the resurrection and the life,—Jesus, who comforted the sisters at Bethany,—Jesus, who had compassion on the weeping widowed mother, who was following the dead body of her only son to the grave, and said to her 'weep not,' gives now the same advice to you; and are not the words precious words? 'Weep not!' you have no real reason to be distressed nor to be gloomy! 'The Lord liveth,' and he undertakes to be your strength and your stay; yea, He also has become your salvation.

> 'Then let not your tears run down,
> Nor your heart with sorrow be riven;
> There's another gem in the Saviour's crown,
> And another saint in Heaven!'

"Your motherless children are all right. The Lord will take care of them. May they always be under the shadow of His wing. I do pray that the all-gracious One may be very near to you and your little ones, and that you may be graciously comforted by Himself. He can comfort as none other can. I know it. I know it from experience. As one whom his mother comforteth, so will He comfort you. May you be drawn nearer to Him. O, the blessedness of coming nigh unto God. Tell Jesus all your trouble, —tell it all to Him. Tell it to Him confidently, and

I know He will be graciously pleased to help you, and to provide for you and your darling little ones: and you shall be able to append your name to the very long list of names already inscribed under the record, penned by the sweet Psalmist of Israel, '*This* poor man cried and the Lord heard *him*, and saved *him* out of all *his* troubles.' . . . . .

"Myself and family present kindest sympathies and affectionate regards, with earnest prayer for your comfort, health, usefulness and everlasting salvation.

"I am yours, very truly,
"HENRY WHEELER."

Mr. Wheeler's daughter, Mrs. George, also writes:

"St. Day, Cornwall,
"November 11th, 1875.

"My dear cousin John,

"I now make my second attempt to write you since I saw the announcement of my dear Agnes's death. I cannot tell you how much I was surprised, nor how full of sorrow my heart was; poor, dear girl! I had always cherished a hope that I should see her again in this world; but our loving Father orders things differently; and knowing, as we do, that what He wills is best, however bitter it may be for us, yet we will strive to say from our hearts, meekly, 'Thy will be done.' Oh, my dear cousin, be it yours to cast your heavy burden at the Saviour's feet. Open to Him those heart sorrows with which no earthly friend can sympathize; He will bear your heavy burden, and you too shall be led to say, 'He doeth all things well.'

"When you feel able to write me a letter of particulars concerning the sad event, I shall feel grateful to you. I should like to know if she was conscious at the time of her death, and what were her last words. Dear girl, I wish I could have seen her, for I had much to talk over with her, but now I must endeavor to meet her in our Father's house. Truly, 'God moves in a mysterious way;' to my earthly eyes it seems as though I could have been better spared than she; there appears to be fewer ties to bind me down here, but she was more meet for the inheritance than I.

"I have often grieved that the correspondence between us had ceased, owing to my not knowing your address after you changed circuits.

"My little Sidney sends love and kisses to each of the dear little ones; and in true cousinly sincerity, I remain,
    "Yours truly,
     "JANE ELEANOR GEORGE."

Rev. C. Spurr, President of our Eastern Conference, wrote as follows from Lowell, Mass:

"Dear brother Acornley,

"I received your card bearing the mournful intelligence of the death of your dear wife. How dreary and lonely you must feel! My wife joins with me in deep sympathy with you in your painful bereavement; and we pray that He in whom you trust may sustain and comfort you in your deep distress and trouble.

"O, that I could say something to soothe your sorrowing heart! But how well I know the inability of mortals to do this. Our warmest sympathy is too cool, and our words too feeble, to reach the depths, and remove the sorrow of a grief stricken heart—a heart ready to burst with anguish by the removal of a loved one, and that loved one, the light of the eyes. I would say, however, in the language of the apostle Paul, 'Sorrow not as those who have no hope, for if we believe that God raised up Jesus from the dead, even so them also that sleep in Jesus will God bring with him.' How sweet the thought! 'she is not dead but sleepeth.' Christ our blessed mediator shall again wake the slumbering clay, remodel it after His own lovely likeness, and the soul shall put it on afresh. Yes, 'He will change the vile body, according to the mighty working whereby He is able to subdue all things to himself.' My brother, let these thoughts cheer you; look to Him from whom cometh all help, and draw from His boundless fullness grace to help in this time of need. I would say more; but it would add nothing to your comfort. May God, the father of all our mercies, comfort you in all your tribulation, and preserve you to His heavenly kingdom, through Jesus Christ our Lord, is the sincere prayer of

"Your brother in Christ,
"CHARLES SPURR."

The Rev. H. G. Russell, Missionary Secretary, wrote from Girardville, Schuylkill Co., Pa:

"Dear brother Acornley,

"Being from home last week, I did not hear of your sore trial until I returned this week, or I would have made an effort to come up to see you. Dear brother, I deeply sympathize with you in your affliction. But what are all human sympathies compared with that of Jesus, which I know you enjoy. Human friendship can only drop a tear or two; but Jesus is *touched* with our feelings. He is eminently *able* to succor the tried ones of his flock, and *willing* to aid them. He is a very present help in time of need. You cannot do better than commit all to the Lord. Your three little ones will be cared for. Oh! to lose a mother's care, no tongue can tell what it is; but the promise is still good, 'As thy day, so shall thy strength be.' 'My grace is sufficient for thee.' 'I will not leave you comfortless.' 'I will come unto you.'

"My wife said, when I came home, 'O! I wish I was near them, so that I could do something for them.' Could you come and spend a week or so with us?

"Dear brother, I find I cannot write. I could talk to you better. I am suffering from a very violent cold; my head pains me. It is with difficulty I pen these few words. May God bless you and your little ones. And by and by may *we* meet her who is gone before, is the prayer of your sincere brother and sister in Christ.

"H. G. and M. RUSSELL."

The Rev. F. Gray, of Pottsville, Schuylkill Co., Pa., says:

"My dear brother,

"I write this in answer to your card, which bore the sad news of your heavy loss. My heart deeply sympathizes with you. I can only commend you to that Being who has been

> 'Our help in ages past,
> Our hope for years to come,
> Our shelter from the stormy blast,
> And our abiding home.'

"Oh! my brother, try and look to God. There is consolation in the words of the apostle, 'We sorrow not as those without hope;' my brother, you have a glorious hope, I pray God may give you enduring grace. 'The Lord is a very present help in trouble.'. 'This poor man cried and the Lord heard him and delivered him out of all his troubles.' This God is your God, and he will be your guide even unto death.

I have no doubt, my brother, on my mind, about your wife's safety; and this is a source of great consolation. Try and reconcile yourself to God's will. 'Thy will, O God, be done!' My father and mother are here on a visit; they wish to be remembered very kindly to you. My heart is full at present; I hope to hear from you as soon as you have an opportunity to write. Connexional committee meets next week. I wish you were able to be with us. I should like to see you, especially just now. The Lord help and bless you for Christ's sake. Regard me as your true friend and well wisher. My wife and parents join with me in love to you and the dear children.

"I am yours in Christ Jesus,

"FRANCIS GRAY."

The Rev. W. B. Bache of Hazelton, Luzerne Co., Pa., says: "My dear brother, put your trust in that Saviour whom you have so earnestly presented to others. I pray that our heavenly Father may support you with his grace, and guide you by his wisdom. O, may he sanctify this providence, and may Christ himself still be the great desire of your heart. Since he has taken away the desire of your eyes, and the helpmeet of your life; may you realize the fulfillment of his promise, 'I am with you always, even unto the end.' Yes, my brother, in joy and in sorrow; in health and affliction; on land and on sea. Oh! what a friend.

"I pray that your three motherless children may be the object of our everlasting Father's love and care. They and you, my dear brother, now need the continued sympathy of Godly friends; and especially that of our never-dying, and ever-living friend, Jesus Christ. May the blessing of Heaven be with you, and the God of Jacob be your refuge. Amen.

"I remain yours, in Him who is the best centre of our love and union, the Lord our righteousness.

"WILLIAM B. BACHE."

Expressions of sympathy were also received from Rev. M. Harvey of Ohltown, Ohio, from Howard Daisley, Esq., book steward, of Brooklyn, N. Y., and many others. An old and valued friend of our youth, in Rochdale, England, wrote as follows :—

"My dear old friend,

. . . . . "I have heard of your great trouble, and I trust you will not take it amiss if I tender you my sincere sympathies in your affliction; even you whose work and duty it is to bind the broken hearted, and speak words of comfort to those in trouble and distress, will perhaps feel encourged by receiving a word of sympathy from an old friend far away. 'All things' (says the good old book) 'work together for good,' to them that love and serve Him. This may be easy to preach; may you have grace given you in this dark hour to feel and realize the truthfulness of its teachings. I pray that it may lead you to greater devotion, and a higher standard of usefulness; and that you may more and more become a workman that needeth not to be ashamed, rightly dividing the word of truth. May the blessing of our common Father be with you, and give you that grace you so much need at present. . . . . .

"If convenient, please write me a few lines, they will be thankfully received. Mrs. Harris joins me in kindest remembrance, with every wish for your future success.

"Truly Yours,

"R. HARRIS."

We felt at this time an uncontrollable longing to see the land of our birth; and having suffered considerably from nervous prostration, and being physically and mentally unwell, we hoped that a voyage across the Atlantic would improve our health. We also thought that if we could place our two eldest children in the care of their grandmother—in compliance with the request of her whom we now mourn—we could return to our work, and spend the residue of our days contentedly in our blessed Master's service. Accordingly, we left the baby with Mr. and Mrs. Tipton, of Morris Run, who kindly cared for him as though he had been their own child, until death snatched him from their embrace. It is impossible for us to *express*, much less *discharge* the obligation we feel for their great kindness, and unwearied and self-sacrificing attentions to us and ours. May the God of all grace ever bless them.

On the 8th of December, 1875, we stepped on board—with two children—the good ship "Algeria," and after ten days, landed in Liverpool; and the same evening were in the midst of our dear friends and relatives. While in England we were the recipient of a great number of letters. An extract or two will illustrate.

The Rev. James Crompton, of Haslingden, says:
"Dear brother,

"I am glad to have a line from you. I saw in the paper an account of the death of your dear wife, and I felt as if an old friend had departed. I truly sympathize with you under your stroke of bereavement. I know well what it is! I should be glad to see you . . . . . try to come as far."

The Rev. M. Shorrock, of Walkden, near Manchester, writes:

"Dear brother Acornley,

. . . . . "I was much pleased to hear from you and to learn that you were at home again; though I deeply regret the *cause*. I was sorry to hear that you had lost your dear wife. I sincerely sympathize with you in your loss. . . . . . . Please let me know when you propose going back, for if you cannot come here I will try to get to Rochdale. Mrs. S. joins me in kind regards to you and your mother and family.

"Yours as ever,

"M. SHORROCK."

Manifestations of kindness and sympathy were also received from Rev. William Harris, of Stockport, Rev. John Mould, of Rochdale, and many others.

We cannot very well finish our task of love without recording extracts from letters received from two of our flock in Morris Run. The first one from Mr. George Palmer, we value, as it comes from one who, at that time was laboring under deep conviction of sin; but who since then has ventured his all on the atonement of Christ, and thus has experienced the blessedness of those whose sins are forgiven. The other is from one who, during our two years stay in Morris Run, showed much kindness to ourself and Mrs. Acornley.

"Dear friend,

"I was glad to hear from you, and hope you are getting better; although I am afraid you are not doing very well, by the letter you wrote Tipton. Dear Mr. Acornley, I don't think you ought to fret about anything; you are on friendly terms with the Lord, and that ought to balance all your troubles. I think I will turn preacher for once, and see how I can preach to you. Now, when I discover that the Lord has freely forgiven me all my sins, it seems to me I should be ashamed to doubt any one single promise in the Bible, and if so, please look at the following: everything 'works together for good to them that love God,' and 'Our light affliction which is but for a moment worketh for us a far more exceeding and eternal weight of glory;' and if you trouble for your children at all remember this, 'Whatsoever ye shall ask the Father in my name, he may give it you.' Again, 'The fervent effectual prayer of a righteous man availeth much.' Now, dear friend, if I was a Christian, I should certainly expect all these promises fulfilled; and should believe the Lord would do just what he says. And I should do just what you have often told me to do, 'trust everything to the Lord.' Dear sir, although I should very much like to see you back again, I hope you won't come back yet, if you think you can get any benefit by staying away. Write again when you get time, and God bless you.

"Yours truly,
"GEORGE PALMER."

"P. S. The reason I wrote in this strain is because I thought you were considerably down when I read Tipton's letter.—G. P."

" Dear brother,

" I am sorry to learn that you are not improving in strength; but hope when this note reaches you,

you will feel better. Dear brother, look to God for your strength, and ask Him to give you mighty faith in His precious promises. He requests you and I to cast our burden upon Him and He will sustain us. Do not suffer past occurrences, trials and difficulties to gloom and injure your future usefulness. God's promises are yea and amen; and everything works for good to those that love Him. Therefore, my dear brother, lay hold on your future engagements with Christian boldness, and ask your heavenly Father to throw light into the dark future, such light as will enable you to steer clear of the rocks in life's ocean. Let your sails be hoisted to the gospel breeze; King Emanuel is your captain, who will lead you at last triumphantly into the port of glory, to join in the melodious chorus of Moses and the Lamb, with those dear ones who have gone before you. May God bless you, dear brother. I pray for you every day, and shall continue to do so.
. . . . . I shall do all that lays in my power to make your home cheerful and pleasant when you return. . . . . . The services of the sanctuary are kept on regularly. The members and the congregation are very anxious to see you return.
. . . . . Cheer up, brother, and buckle on both temporal and spiritual harness. Take your position in the ranks of your King's army, with a manly spirit, and as a valiant soldier of the cross. . . . .

"Yours, as ever, faithful,
"WILLIAM C. JENKINS."

We must now stay our hand. Our task of love is done. May it not be in vain; may the writer and reader finally meet the sainted one—whose life picture we have feebly attempted to draw—in the "Bright forever." Amen.

" Let sorrow now no more prevail to rob my soul of peace;
The longest night will end in day, and all my trials cease:
No tear bedims the golden courts where I shall soon appear—
'In heaven above, where all is love, there'll be no sorrow there!'

God of all comfort! let this truth Thy suffering pilgrims cheer;
Soon shall we reach our heavenly home; each day it draws more near.
When feeble sight no comfort views, let faith the truth declare—
'In heaven above, where all is love, there'll be no sorrow there!'"

THE END.